THE
ADVENTURES
OF A
TRAIN
TREKKER

**ONE LADY'S JOURNEYS ON THE INDIAN PACIFIC AND
THE GHAN AND TALES OF QUEENSLAND RAIL**

ADRIANA CARBONI

Published by Adriana Carboni
In Partnership with Great Writers Media

 Great Writers Media

Great Writers Media
Email: info@greatwritersmedia.com
Phone: 877-556-0487

ISBN: 979-8-89175-040-1 (sc)
ISBN: 979-8-89175-053-1 (hb)
ISBN: 979-8-89175-041-8 (ebk)

I would like to thank my dear friend Judy Ley for her invaluable contribution to this book.

Adriana
Sydney
2024

CONTENTS

CHAPTER 1

The Beginning

From the dawn of railways, there have been people fascinated with the technology of trains, their design, and their construction that made rail travel possible in difficult terrain. Today many people travel over great distances to see or ride particular trains and lines or to visit museums. Since their beginning, railways have been about more than just transporting goods and people from one place to another. The puffing of the earliest steam locomotives captivated the cities and towns whenever they arrived and today the sheer strength of freight trains, the movement and streamlined appearance of modern high speed rail or the modern marvels of engineering that are train stations, bridges, tunnels or marshalling yards are a sight to behold, and a reason for tourism. You don't have to be a fanatic listing numbers and dates of train sightings in a book to appreciate the qualities and fascination that is rail travel and everything associated with it. Railroads continue to applaud the natural beauty of the landscapes traversed or the cities served even if the speed is nothing to write home about.

I have always been fascinated by long distance train travel. It was about twenty years ago when I saw a documentary about Great Southern Railways, that I decided a journey on the Indian Pacific would be the trip of a lifetime. It didn't occur to me then, but, long distance train travel would become almost an obsession with me. This would continue on to the famous Ghan train. Railway stations have always attracted me, not just because the trains are there, but because they echo the completed journey and shrill with the sad noises of departure. The enthusiasm for trains and railways is, I have been told, incurable – the fascination of vehicles that run on rails!

The first time I was about to experience a long-distance train journey, I didn't know what to expect. It was Sydney to Perth, on the Indian Pacific, a distance of 4352 kilometres – four days and three nights!

Why is it called the Indian Pacific? Appropriately named because it travels from East to West, from the Pacific Ocean to the Indian Ocean and visa versa, one of the longest train journeys in the world. At that time the Indian Pacific left Sydney twice a week, and it was on a Wednesday that I boarded the 1400 tonne mighty train which was scheduled to depart at 3.15pm. Shortly before 3pm I pinched myself as I heard the announcement: "will passengers for the Indian Pacific calling at Broken Hill, Adelaide and Perth, please make their way to platforms 2 and 3". The train was so long it needed two platforms, though it came together just outside the station. I checked in and took my luggage on board with me to be stored in my own single compartment. It was amazing how they fitted everything into a small space, the bed folded into an armchair, the wash basin into the wall, and there was a cupboard for your clothes and an overhead shelf. Showers were positioned at the end of the carriage. A complimentary toiletries bag was provided with shampoo, conditioner, moisturizer, tissues and hand cream. My suitcase was placed under the bed. Almost immediately the cabin steward came to tell me about breakfast, lunch and dinner times. I selected an early dinner (the first meal that day). Little did I know that I would have to have an early breakfast to suit the next morning at 6:30. 6:30 BREAKFAST! Hey, I'm on holidays! I soon learned the system – late dinner, late breakfast!

There was music and pre-boarding snacks and cheery uniformed staff to welcome everyone on board and present a few ground rules, "you don't want to mess with the steward's restaurant seating plans", as I contemplated what lay ahead - the greatest of Australia's long-distance train journeys. I eyed other passengers, almost overwhelmingly Australians and stepping aboard the train I felt a great sense of anticipation as this unforgettable Australian adventure began to unfold. Although there were mainly Australians on board, I met an English couple on an extensive tour of the country who loved ticking off exotic-sounding place names on the map – Wirraminna, Orange East Fork, Mambray Creek, and West Kalgoorlie, and marveling at the fact that at times, so flat was the surrounding country that they could actually see the curvature of the earth! Mealtimes also afforded the opportunity to break the day and discover more about my fellow passengers. Some, as the journey progressed, revealed that they were in fact direct descendants of the early convicts. Others were train enthusiasts and for some, their first long distance journey. Entertainment came in the form of board games and books to borrow, and regular performances by the on-board guitar player.

We left on time and travelled west at an average speed of 85km through the picturesque World Heritage Area of the Blue Mountains, about one hundred kilometres from Sydney.

From inside the cabin I was touched by the vast beauty of this magnificent country – the textures, the light, the unimaginable hues. I settled into my cabin and spent the afternoon taking in the scenery as it transformed from skyscrapers and traffic lights to the forested valleys of the stunning Blue Mountains. There was no stop at the Mountains on the way over to Perth, however, on the way back there were excursions.

Continuing on, we passed Lithgow, Bathurst, Orange, Parkes, Condobolin and Ivanhoe. Lithgow is situated in the Central Tablelands of New South Wales located on the Great Western Highway, about 150 kilometres west of Sydney. The town is surrounded by a varied landscape which includes national parks, one of which, the Blue Mountains National Park, is a world heritage area. There is The Wollemi National Park which is home to the Jurassic-age tree the Wollemi Pine, after which the park was named.

Bathurst was the next town we passed. Bathurst is often referred to as the Gold Country as it was the site of the first gold discovery and where the first gold rush occurred in Australia. Today education, tourism and manufacturing propel the economy. The internationally known racetrack Mount Panorama is a landmark of the city and it is best known as the home of the Bathurst 1000 motor race held each October, and the Bathurst 12 Hour event held each February. The track is a 6,213 kilometre long street circuit, which is used as a public road on non-race days. The National Motor Racing Museum located next to the track, holds an interesting exhibition of Motor Racing.

Next we passed Orange, which is the birthplace of poets Banjo Paterson and Kenneth Slessor, although, Paterson lived in Orange for only a short time as an infant. A significant nearby landmark is Mount Canobolas with a peak elevation of 1,395 metres and commanding views of the district. Orange is situated within the traditional lands of the Wiradjuri people who are scattered throughout central New South Wales and have survived as skilled hunter-fisher-gatherers, in family groups or clans and many still use knowledge of hunting and gathering techniques as part of their customary life.

As we travelled further through the Central West of New South Wales we passed the town of Parkes which is part of the traditional lands of the Wiradjuri people, who have lived on the lands of the three rivers, including the Lachlan River, for more than 40,000 years. The town was originally called Currajong and in August 1873, Henry Parkes (later Sir Henry), who is recognized as having played an instrumental role in Australia becoming a united and federated country, visited the area. In December 1873 the town was officially renamed Parkes in his honour.

Parkes is home to the radio telescope and has had an important role in the scientific community. In addition to local research, Parkes scientists have assisted NASA for several missions as a Southern Hemisphere relay and communications station. It played an important part in the 1969 Apollo 11 moon landing. When Buzz Aldrin turned on the TV camera on the Lunar Module, three tracking antennas received the signals simultaneously - Goldstone in California, Honeysuckle Creek near Canberra, and the 64 metre dish at Parkes. Since they started the spacewalk early, the Moon was only just above the horizon and below the visibility of the main Parkes receiver. Although they were able to pick up a quality signal from the off- axis receiver, the international broadcast alternated between signals from Goldstone and Honeysuckle Creek, the latter of which ultimately broadcast Neil Armstrong's first steps on the Moon worldwide. A little under nine minutes into the broadcast, the Moon rose far enough to be picked up by the main antenna and the international broadcast switched to the Parkes signal. The quality of the TV pictures from Parkes was so superior, that NASA stayed with Parkes as the source of the remainder of the 2.5 hour TV broadcast. The Australian movie, The Dish, starring Sam Neil, is based on that mission.

The on-board radio includes an audio commentary option, and as the sun set behind the mountain ranges you begin to enter the more arid regions of New South Wales. There's a lot of outback, and hours are spent on the train peering into the vast empty space of the wilderness punctuated by the odd shrub and bush and, to everybody's delight, sightings of kangaroos, wallabies and emus. The feeling of desolation is heightened later in the journey on the Nullarbor Plain, that huge expanse of arid flat terrain. In writing about Edward John Eyre's voyages (Eyre was the first European to cross the Nullarbor), Henry Kingsley, an English novelist, wrote that Eyre described the area across the Nullarbor and the Great Australian Bight as a "hideous anomaly, a blot on the face of nature, the sort of place one gets into in bad dreams" (Eyre, Edward, (para.6) states that…"A hideous anomaly"). Some friends had warned me – "you might find it monotonous." Actually no, I found the starkness and extraordinary flatness of the scenery spellbinding, oddly arousing and utterly other-worldly. Although I had been on Australia's other epic train journey – the Ghan that went from Adelaide to Darwin I was never bored. The two books I took with me were never opened! As a Gold Class traveller, I found myself sharing tables with others for almost every meal – something that without exception I found enjoyable, although the separate dining arrangements afforded to guests in the superior Platinum Class carriages, were outstanding. Entertainment came in the form of performances by the on-board guitar player Warren. That evening I went to bed and quickly fell asleep as the train rolled soothingly onwards.

The next stop was Broken Hill early the next morning and being so early nothing much was open. However, on the way back to Sydney we arrived in the afternoon, enough time for an off-train excursion. We passed the small town of Peterborough, which was settled to service the agricultural and pastoral efforts of the 1870s. It is an historical railway town on the southern edge of the Flinders Ranges, located 246 kilometres north of Adelaide via Gawler and Burra. I was lucky enough to visit the quaint town of Peterborough when, along with some friends I drove from Sydney to Adelaide (overnight at Broken Hill).

Mr. William Heithersay was the first person to start a business venture, a blacksmith's shop, and soon other people followed in establishing businesses. The railways have been unbelievably important to the district, with the town being significant in linking north, south, east and west. The carriage of ore from Broken Hill to the smelters at Port Pirie was the major contributor to rail traffic through Peterborough, with 70 trains per day being reported in October 1898. It wasn't just freight and ore which passed through Peterborough, the Old Ghan did from 1929 with the original narrow gauge tracks still in place.

The first transcontinental railway, Brisbane to Perth, started passing through Peterborough from 1917, and the first Indian Pacific passenger express did so too from February 1970, and continues to do so today. Unfortunately the railways have all but left the town, however the properties and memories of that great steam era had been preserved at the Steamtown Heritage Rail Centre in the town. There are two possible explanations for the name, the first maintains that it was named after Peters Store – the first general store in the town, and the second more widely accepted, claims that Peter Doeche, who owned the land upon which the town was built, decided to divide his land and sell it at auction. By the end of the first day he had sold 33 acres for £1700. To honour this remarkable achievement the town was named after Doecke and became 'Petersburg'. In 1917, when anti-German sentiment was at its height, the town's name, which sounded too German, was changed to Peterborough. Launched in 1977 the Steamtown Heritage Rail Centre was originally created to run a steam train service between Peterborough and Quorn with rolling stock dating from the 1920s. It was designed to provide visitors with the experience of an old-style railway journey. Today it focuses on the memories of the town's impressive railway history. The Town Carriage Museum which is also the local Visitor Information Centre, is a unique use of an old first class sleeping carriage dating from 1917. There are eighteen glass case displays which represent events in the town's history, people of significance and aspects of life in the town.

Located in a small park in front of the Visitor Centre is Bob the Railway Dog, a sculpture by South Australian sculptor, Silvio Apponyi. Bob is the one of the best known dogs in Australia and he passed his whole life on a train, his favourite seat being on top of a coal box. In this way he had travelled many thousands of kilometres, going all over the lines in South Australia. He was well known in Victoria, frequently seen in Sydney and had been up as far as Brisbane.

The most strange part of his behaviour is that he had no master, but every engine driver was his friend. At night he would follow home his engine man of the day never leaving him or letting him out of his sight until they were back at the Railway Station in the morning, when he started off on another of his endless journeys. The inscription on the sculpture explains: "The story of Bob, railway mascot, begins when he was rounded up in Adelaide in 1883 with a lot of other stray dogs being sent north to the rabbit plague. He was adopted by railway guard William Ferry of Terowie and a few months later moved with him to Peterborough. Bob began travelling on trains, first with his owner and then on his own. He jumped on and off trains as the mood took him making interstate journeys and short suburban trips on trams as well as trains (he also made river trips on the Murray Steamers). He travelled far – to Sydney and Melbourne, Oodnadatta, Broken Hill, Mt Gambier and more. When he died in 1895 he was mourned by the travelling public all over Australia".

While busy exploring Adelaide on a previous visit to South Australia, I visited a town that I had not been to before. That was Burra, 160 kilometres north-east of Adelaide along the Barrier Highway. Burra became a thriving mining community with the discovery of copper in 1845, and by 1850 the town was Australia's largest inland settlement. The Burra mines and related buildings are the earliest examples of Cornish mining and domestic architecture in South Australia. Once copper production slowed in the 1870s, Burra evolved into a service centre, and the rise of a successful merino industry, made Burra a centre for sheep-breeding and brought further prosperity to the town. The quickest way to get there is by bus. The journey time is around 3 hours 15 minutes from Adelaide and covers a distance of around 183 kilometres. Burra which calls itself 'An Historic Copper Town and the Merino Capital of the World', is a unique township.

It was declared a State Heritage town in 1994 because of its many outstanding historic buildings and the opportunity it offers for the visitor to understand a little of what life was like in a 19th century copper mining town. There is considerable debate about the origin of the word "burra". Some claim that

it comes from a Hindustani expression "burra burra" meaning "great great" and was used by shepherds who came from India to work in the area. Others claim that it is of Aboriginal origin which appears in words like kookaburra and Tibooburra. Another interpretation is that burra burra was used by miners from Devon. I stayed in one of the converted miners cottages and I was so impressed that I stayed a week. Great cottages, well appointed, lovely gardens, clean, comfortable, a plentiful breakfast and underfloor heating in the bathroom. What more could you want? I was introduced to a local historian who, telling me the traditionalism, explained how different areas of the town had become little ghettos of British miners. "It is worth noting that Burra was a uniquely segregated community with Redruth for the Cornish miners, Aberdeen for the Scottish miners, Llychwr for the Welsh miners" (Aussie Towns, (ND. Para.17), states that…"It is worth noting that

Burra was uniquely segregated…"), the historian explained as he showed me around the ruins of Hampton (an English style township on the outskirts of Burra, the stone ruins and foundations are the only remains of the former township of Hampton Village, once a bustling settlement during the peak mining period in Burra from the 1860s). Climbing through the rubble gave me an understanding of the miners' lives.

A must do for railway enthusiasts is a trip on the historic restored steam or heritage diesel train journey from Port Augusta to Quorn, following part of the famous Old Ghan Railway line through Pichi Richi pass to Quorn. Gum-lined creeks, bluebush-studded hills and ancient rocky outcrops roll past at the relaxed pace of years gone by. Great photo opportunities.

The Morphett Engine House Museum is a remarkable National Trust building first constructed in 1858, and was gutted by fire in 1925 and fully restored in 1986. Visitors can walk through an underground adit and view the mineshaft, as well as gain access to Morphett's Windinghouse, mine offices and cottages, Grave's Enginhouse and a view of an open-cut mine. The collection includes a scale model of a jinker, mining artefacts, an 1820s pocket bible and quality samples of malachite and azurite (two forms of copper ore mined on the site).

Before European settlement, the Ngadjuri Aboriginal people inhabited the area, and their first Western contact was in 1839, when squatter William Peter arrived. Pastoralists grazed much of the Ngadjuri land from the 1840s and, although there was conflict, Ngadjuri people worked as shepherds and wool scourers, particularly once the area was emptied during the gold rushes of the 1850s. Their population was seriously exhausted by introduced European diseases and they were reported to be extinct 1878. Vestiges of their culture remain with rock art and burial sites in the area and some people are able to claim Ngadjuri ancestry.

After Peterborough, we passed Clare, a town in the delightful secluded Clare Valley, where, if you visit one day, you'll fall in love with the Valley's tempting country pubs, not to mention the wineries, famous for Riesling. If you're in the area, as I was some years before, take a detour and visit Clare, you won't be disappointed.

Well then, back to the train for a LATE breakfast! After breakfast one can sit in the lounge car and order drinks from the well-stocked bar. Later, an exquisite lunch and the very best of Australian wines were served in the dining car. After lunch it was back to the lounge car where one can chat and make new friends, mostly Australians from every part of the country. Dinner time came around quickly – I think I had worn out the floor going back and forth to and from my compartment! The corridors were narrow, so, one had to stand firmly against the wall to let another person pass, thew! You hope that you don't meet a large person.

CHAPTER 2

Adelaide and the Nullarbor

We arrived in Adelaide at 4.00pm the next day and stayed for two hours. There was an excursion around the city, which is known as the city of churches and it has the river Torrens with beautiful and well kept gardens along the banks. Initially the name, City of Churches, was because of the quantity of churches, but the name shows that ever since South Australia was colonized, a large number of religions have been freely practised in the state, setting it apart from the other capital cities as an inspiration of religious tolerance. I have visited Adelaide numerous times, and the more I visited, the more I enjoyed this lovely city. Adelaide's parklands span 760 hectares – twice the area of New York City's Central Park. A step away from the city streets is a veritable Garden of Eden with blooming rose gardens, tropical sanctuaries, rambling yet manicured gardens and lush lawns perfect for picnicking – the Adelaide Botanic Gardens.

A ride on the Cockle Train, a superb old steam train, which travels between Goolwa and the ocean wharfs at Port Elliot and Victor Harbor, is a pleasure not to be missed. The journey takes 30 minutes and it runs at different times of the year. Goolwa an historic port at the mouth of the Murray River, is now an upmarket holiday resort for Adelaide people and is only an hour's drive from the Adelaide CBD. Goolwa is an important location which offers visitors a series of experiences ranging from the development of the port near the mouth of the Murray River; to an insight into the importance of the River as a transport route prior to the construction of railway lines.

A popular tourist destination I visited was Victor Harbor (despite the fact that harbour is normally spelt with a "u" in modern Australian English, the name of the city is spelt Victor Harbor. This spelling, found in several geographical names in South Australia, including Outer Harbor, is the result of spelling errors made by an early Surveyor General of South Australia). It is situated on the coast of the Fleurieu Peninsula, about 80 kilometres south of Adelaide. I treated myself and stayed overnight at the McCracken Country Club which is the ideal place for leisure, dining, golf and relaxation.

Victor Harbor was originally home to the Ramindjeri people, who hunted and gathered in the region they called 'Wirramulla' for thousands of years prior to European settlement in 1802. The fertile lands sustained huge animal populations while the waters were sheltered and abundant with life.

After South Australia was colonized in 1826, the peninsula started exporting whale oil, where the produce was exported by sea. But as navigating the Murray Mouth became difficult and dangerous for steamers, a decision was made to build a railway. For many years goods were conveyed between the mainland and the island on railway trucks drawn by horses, which were used instead of steam engines to contain costs. As the Causeway became popular, the South Australian Railways decided to utilize one of their unused horse-drawn passenger transport to offer a service to the island, and in 1894 the passenger horse tramway was established.

The Coral Street Art Space encourages the development of a creative cultural industry in Victor Harbor by providing a meeting place for local artists, community members and groups, where they can work, exhibit, and share their experiences.

The Victor Harbor Beachside Markets, open two Sundays a month, has plenty to see and do. The Esplanade comes alive with stall holders setting up their wares, selling anything from bric-a-brac to fashion, tools, beauty products, hot food, coffee and plenty more. A visit here added to my Victor Harbor enjoyable experience (not to mention shopping).

One of the favourite activities for visitors here is to hitch a ride on the horse-drawn tram over a 630-metre long wooden causeway connecting the nearby Granite Island. Granite Island is distinguished by the huge granite boulders tinged with orange moss, with sound of waves crashing against the rocky shore – a stirring soundtrack to your visit. Kaiki, the indigenous name for Granite Island, has a great spiritual significance as does the southern right whale, the largest whale, with the local aboriginal population.

This small island is home to a large colony of Little Penguins which shelter on the island during the night, departing in the morning to hunt for fish before returning at sunset. The penguins generally spend the day out in the ocean and the night in their nests, so the best time to see them is at dusk when they return from their escapades out at sea. Be sure to keep your distance from them and their burrows – penguins are delicate creatures and even the slightest change of scent to their surroundings has been known to change the way they behave and cause them to abandon their burrows and breeding activity completely. Little Penguins once had few predators, however, introduced foxes, rats and domestic cats and dogs soon became a major menace to coastal populations. For safety reasons dogs, cats and other species are not allowed on the island.

A team of Clydesdale horses pull the carriages and is one of the very few horse-drawn tram routes remaining in public transit service. You would be mistaken for thinking that the horses are badly done by – having to pull a heavy tram all that way, however, the trams run on roller bearings, making it easy for the horses by not having to strain. The horses are well looked after and treated with kindness. A spokesperson said that the horse drawn tram employees have the relevant skills, knowledge and experience to perform their duties relevant to their employment. Due to its unusual granite formations, Granite Island Recreation Park of 62 acres, is one of the most recognized ecological attractions in Victor Harbor.

The mighty Murray River is one of the world's longest navigable rivers and stretches 2,700 kilometres from the mountains of the Great Dividing Range in north-eastern Victoria to near Adelaide in South Australia. You can join the intimate cruising vessel, the Proud Mary to discover the Murray River's eco-system at its best. Since ancient times Aboriginal people have lived along the river and, after European settlement, the river was travelled by some of Australia's earliest European explorers. Only a 45 minute drive from Adelaide it embarks and disembarks guests from Murray Bridge. You have a choice of a number of cruising vessels which take you on a peaceful, relaxing journey passing beautiful Murray River landscapes. One of the greatest things I took away from the cruise, was an appreciation of the River's intrinsic value to Australia's culture and meaning.

Before Europeans arrived, the Kaurna tribe lived in the Adelaide area. The Australian Aborigines called the Adelaide area Tandanya, "the place of the red kangaroo" (Adelaida, (ND. Para. 1) states that…."Tandanya is a word in the Kaurna language that means 'Red Kangaroo Place")), (Surveyor-general William Light selected the site for the capital of the new colony of South Australia, in December 1836), and it was named after the wife of King George IV.

At first the settlers were British or Irish but in the mid-19th century many Germans settled in Adelaide and the surrounding area. The German settlers were mostly Lutherans escaping persecution by the King of Prussia.

The town of Hahndorf in the lush landscape of the Adelaide Hills, was home to these early settlers who thrived in their farming roles and brought many German nuances to the area. This old-fashioned village oozes Bavarian charm, with plenty of pubs, cafes, and artisan shops to enjoy; shops – my weakness! Today, Hahndorf, the oldest surviving German settlement in Australia, is not only a popular tourist attraction, but it is also an important part of Australia's lengthy relatively great history. Only a 20-minute car ride from Adelaide, Hahndorf's close proximity to the city means that taxis are a viable transport option for those who prefer it to driving or public transport. I went on a guided sightseeing tour, which was most enjoyable and a stress-free way to discover everything there is to know about Hahndorf. I especially liked the soft, decadent, creamy fudge made in Hahndorf, which is home to some of the most delicious pieces of sweets. One of the things that Germany is famous for, is its beer, and there are plenty of artisan beer and winery outlets along the main street, while the surrounding rolling hills are peppered with vineyards packed with unique flavours. One of the most popular attractions in Hahndorf is the Beerenberg Farm which dates back to the early 1800s. It has been run by five generations of the Paech family since the German immigrants settled in this part of the country. The working farm produces tonnes of goods every year, including strawberries, mixed vegetables, sweetcorn, jams (my favourite is the fig and almond jam – yummy), pickles, chutneys and sauces. Museums and galleries are aplenty; the German Migration Museum and the Hahndorf Academy are worth a visit to gain insight to the history and culture of the town. For over 50 years, The Cedars was home to Sir Hans Heysen, a local artist in Hahndorf. Today it is an historic house that showcases some of his finest works. Throughout the immaculately kept house, the studio and gardens, you can get to appreciate Heysen, who was renowned for his diverse techniques and his variety of subject matter. A visit to Hahndorf is not complete without a wander down the main street, which is alight with charming cafes, traditional restaurants, pubs that recollect the historic Germanic life, filled with food, drinks, art, and culture. While in town, I savoured some delectable ice cream at the Ye Olde Ice Creamery. They have 25 flavours, the most popular being Fig and Almond, Rum and Raisin, Salted Caramel, Persian Pistachio, Peanut Butter Caramel and exotic ones like Durian and Taro. Hahndorf is a lovely place full of art, history, art exhibitions and museums.

In 1900 the population of Adelaide was 162,000 and it was growing rapidly. In 1906 the statue of William Light was unveiled. I visited Adelaide's north-eastern suburbs where traditional Italian families go about their business as if they were a hemisphere away! I uncovered the best of this unique corner of the city – our own "dolce vita". I took a trip out to the Adelaide Hills from where you get a great panoramic view of the city. The majestic peaks of the Mount Lofty Ranges provide views across Adelaide's city skyline to the coast. More than 350,000 people per year visit the peaks which rise more than 727 metres above sea level.

I explored the Torrens River on a pedal powered boat on the day. The Migration Museum works towards understanding and enjoyment of South Australia's diverse cultures. It is a place to discover the many identities of the people of South Australia through the stories of individuals and communities.

Glenelg Beach is Adelaide's most popular city beach, offering an exciting feeling and great atmosphere for all to enjoy. It is well known for its wide beach, stunning sunsets, rich heritage and bustling shops, sidewalk cafes and loads of entertainment. The Adelaide-Himeji Garden is worth a visit, it contains features which are of profound religious significance to the Japanese people. It has features designed to recollect the beauty of nature. The Tandanya is the leading Aboriginal and Torres Strait Islander arts and Culltural organization nationally. Without doubt Tandanya has demonstrated a capacity to display artists' work and promoting artistic development from production to exhibition and facilitates sales through exhibition of work within its galleries and Gallery Shop as well as through ticketed and non-ticketed Festival performances within the Tandanya Theatre. If you're fortunate enough to be there during a performing season, you will be delighted.

If it's a bit of a tipple you're after, speakeasy bars run through the city like the lifeblood for thirsty merrymakers. There are boutiques concealed under the streets, expensive watering holes perched above the city skyline, laneways brimming with cocktail lounges and unique bars hidden behind unpretentious walls.

The Adelaide Central Market which offers a huge range of fresh food including fruit and vegetables, meat, poultry, seafood, cheeses bakery, smallgoods and health foods, is one of the largest undercover fresh produce markets in the Southern Hemisphere. It certainly merits a visit and has some of the most frequented cafes and eateries in Adelaide.

Less than an hour's drive from Adelaide are the world-famous Adelaide Hills, Barossa and McLaren Vale wine regions. The Barossa Valley is located 60km from Adelaide, so there is no time for an excursion. On another occasion I left the train and spent a week or so there visiting among other things the wineries - please watch your intake of wine; a little sip here and there can become overwhelming – cheers! The Barossa is also known for its range of small goods, cheeses and dried fruits. It has strong European ties having been populated by German and Cornish settlers in the 1840s. Most farming implements were distinctively German, the best known being the German wagon which was used for everything, from family coach to wedding coach, hearse, hay carrier, heavy transport, caravan, grape carrier and water cart. What a handy thing to have! The Barossa Valley is a natural valley perfect for wine making, and this was due to the local Aboriginal communities setting off fires annually away from the undergrowth. Tanunda is undoubtedly the biggest tourist stop in the valley and is the focal point for activities and attractions including delicious restaurants.

One of the best known wine producers, Joseph Ernst Seppelt, arrived from Silesia in 1850, with his wife Charlotte, his two sons, daughter, thirteen families and a group of young men who had worked for him. After first settling at Klemzig, the family later moved to Seppeltsfield where Joseph grew tobacco, wheat and wine. By the mid 1860s he began constructing a full-scale winery plant which was continued, after his death in 1868 by his son Benno.

Of course when you mention great Australian wines, Penfolds always comes to mind. It's 15 minutes away from the Adelaide CBD in the beautiful foothills. You can sip and savour their best drops and then allow yourself a sumptuous meal at the Penfolds Magill Estate. With breathtaking views over the vineyards and Adelaide city, this multi award-winning restaurant is one of the favourite spots to settle in for a decadent dinner. A votre santè!

Arguably the best sports stadium in Australia, nothing compares to the excitement and pleasure of watching a game at the Adelaide oval. Grab the best seats in the house and see the sun set from the best vantage point in Adelaide.

If you are an animal lover, a visit to the Adelaide Zoo should be on your itinerary, even if only to see the only pair of Giant Pandas in the Southern Hemisphere, Wang Wang and Fu Ni. This lush oasis is home to animals from all over the world as well as Australia's most iconic species.

The North Terrace is home to innumerable art galleries and museums. Visit the Art Gallery of South Australia housing one of the country's best art collections and exhibitions. Next you'll find the South Australian Museum, famous for its world-class natural history and cultural collections. If you require more art therapy, the University of South Australia's Samstag Museum of Art displays works from South Australian artists as well as a magnificent collection of Aboriginal bark paintings.

The award winning Wadlata Outback Centre at 41 Flinders Terrace is very much worth a visit. "Wadlata" is an

Aboriginal word which means to "teach or communicate" (Ausemade, (ND.), states that...... "wadlata is an Aboriginal Parnkhalia' word which means to "teach or communicate"). An absorbing lesson in "The Outback Tunnel of Time", begins with a virtual journey 15 million years ago when dinosaurs roamed the land. You discover the evolution of the Australian Outback and the Flinders Ranges while listening to Aboriginal stories, follow Akurra the rainbow serpent, back to the times when the land was created. Watch films, for example "Back of Beyond" about the Birdsville Track mailman Tom Kruse, and enjoy the interactive displays about the Australian Outback and the ancient continent that is Australia.

As remote mail carrier in outback South Australia, Peter 'Rowie' Rowe has travelled distances most posties can only dream about. Mr. Rowe said over the last 15 years he had fallen in love with the rugged, sunburnt country he traversed, collecting many friendships and memories along the way. Running out of the iconic opal mining town of Coober Pedy, his 600 kilometres round-trip runs twice a week to five remote pastoral stations along the historic Oodnadatta track, including the world's largest cattle station on Anna Creek. The route follows in the steps of famous explorers like John McDouall Stuart and takes him past hidden gems such as the old Ghan railway line, the Overland Telegraph Line and Australia's first solar-powered telephone in William Creek. "Every day I travel through the country that I love and I meet up with all my friends", he said. Rowie offers a special outback experience for tourists who ride along with him on his mail route from Oodnadatta to William Creek, as he shares his affection for outback flora and fauna, the history of the early explorers and the arid land pastoral industry. "I also carry paying passengers, so, I meet people from all different walks of life", he said (Rowe, Peter, (2007 para. 3), states that...."every day I travel...").

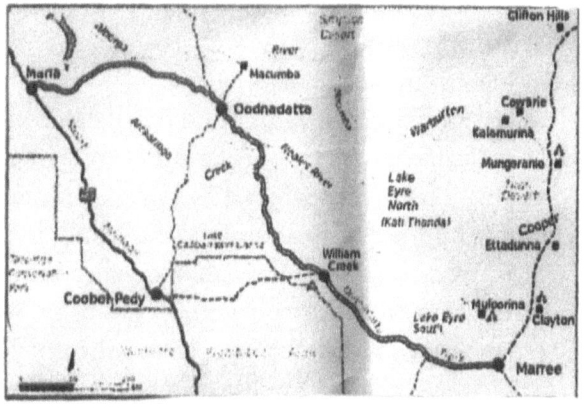

We passed Port Pirie, which is 223 kilometres north of Adelaide on the upper Spencer Gulf is known as The City of Friendly People. It has extensive history which dates back to 1845 and was the first proclaimed regional city in South Australia. The city's economy is influenced by one of the world's largest lead smelters. As well as lead, it also produces refined silver, zinc, copper and gold. When Samuel Germein found the creek upon which Port Pirie developed it became know as Samuel's Creek. Then, in 1845, a schooner named John Pirie travelled up the creek, loaded a flock of sheep and transported them to Port Lincoln. This lead the South Australian governor, Governor Robe, to name the settlement Port Pirie, after John Pirie, a director of a South Australian Company.

Kangaroo Island

Just 25 minutes away by air and 2.5 hours by ferry is Kangaroo Island. I had heard of postcard-perfect beaches, but seeing is believing – these beaches must be some of the best in Australia. This secluded pocket of island hinterland presents some of the most authentic nature experiences in

Australia. Cross over ancient landscapes moulded by time and get within a whisker of iconic Australian animals. I started ticking off my bucket list!

The first European explorers found the island to be uninhabited, as indicated by the lack of campfires and tameness of the wildlife, until the 1930s when Aboriginal campsites were discovered in a number of areas around the island, including one near the fur seal colony of Cape du Couedic. After a long period of seclusion from human contact, Kangaroo Island experienced a series of visits by people of different nationalities in quick succession. English, French and American sailors visited in 1802, 1803 and 1804 respectively. The first were an English crew onboard The Investigator. They were delighted when they discovered and consumed large numbers of unsuspecting kangaroos on the shore. Their commander, Captain Matthew Flinders, recorded in his log, "… in gratitude for so seasonable a supply, I named this southern land Kangaroo Island" (Flinders, Matthew, (1802, para. 3) states that......."in gratitude for so seasonal a supply...."). When the Investigator left, it continued east and at what is now called Encounter Bay, met a French ship commanded by Nicolas Baudin. The two Captains, despite France and England being at war, possessed passports from their opposing administrations, dined together peacefully and shared much information. Their shared intelligence resulted in the French learning about Kangaroo Island, its tasty kangaroos, and good water available right on the shoreline. Their visit soon after included a circumnavigation of the island and the first recorded exploration of the southern coastline. As a result of the French connection, placenames such as Vivonne Bay and Cape du Couedic are seen today. The subsequent discovery of "The place for fat meat 1800" carved in a large tree on the Cygnet River, shows that other English-speaking visitors had beaten Flinders to claim first visiting rights.

Due to rising sea levels, Kangaroo Island was separated from mainland Australia around 10,000 years ago. Recognised as Karta or "Island of the Dead" by mainland Aboriginal tribes, the existence of shells and stone tools demonstrated that Aboriginal people had lived on Kangaroo Island for 16,000 years and might have only disappeared from the island as recently as 2000 years ago.

The wind-blasted boulders of Remarkable Rocks are synonymous with Kangaroo Island. This geological phenomenon has been created from granite by the pounding wind, sea and rain over 500 million years (give or take a million or two?) and is one of the most recognizable landmarks on the island. This "photo opportunity" landscape is tucked within the wilderness of Flinders Chase National Park, with commanding views over the Southern Ocean. Mornings and late afternoons are the best times to visit as the sun transposes the lichen covered rocks into radiant landmarks of Mother Nature's craftmanship. Just a little further down the coast in another geological masterpiece, Admirals Arch which is a natural rock arch carved out over thousands of years by the unrelenting forces of the sea. Stalactites embellish the time-weathered rock formation and frame the roaring Southern Ocean beyond, and the waters below are a haven for New Zealand fur seals who sunbake at the water's edge and folic in the shallow rockpools. Wildlife lovers will also often be rewarded with sightings of dolphins, whales and unique birdlife. The ancient Enchanted Fig Tree, planted about 120 years ago to sustain the first settlers of the island, provides a magical dining experience deserving of a fairytale. From progressive long lunches to decadent dinners dished up by some of South Australia's best chefs including Simon Bryant and Africola's Duncan Welgemoed, the Enchanted Fig Tree is the ultimate dining experience.

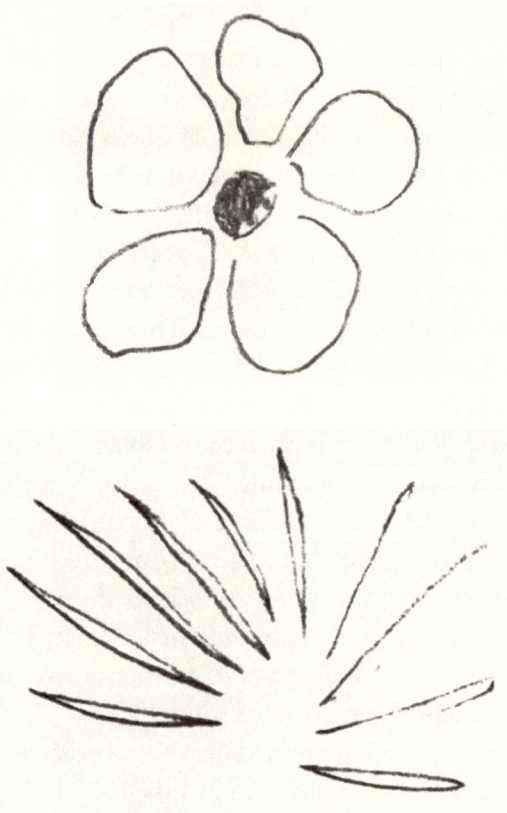

We passed Port Augusta, on the east coast of the Spencer Gulf formerly a seaport, and is now a road traffic and railway junction. It is the fifth largest city in South Australia, and makes it the ideal place for travellers to explore the attractions of Port Augusta and the surrounding areas, the Flinders Ranges for example. The city is known as the "cross roads of Australia" because of its strategic position at the junction of three major Australian highways, and two railway lines. The Spencer Gulf is a natural harbour, discovered by Alexander Elder while aboard the schooner Yatala, captained by Edward Dowsett. The port was named after Augusta Sophia Lady Young, the wife of the Governor of South Australia, Sir

Henry Edward Fox Young. Other major industries up until the mid-2010s, included electricity generation. At June 2018, the estimated urban population was 13,799, having declined over the preceding five years primarily due to cutbacks in public sector employment. Luckily, the government decided to build the Transcontinental railway across the Nullarbor to Perth, and established the railway headquarters in Port Augusta. The town benefited from the railway ever since. Today, Port Augusta is an industrial city with the huge power plant burning the brown coal from Leigh Creek, and supplying about 40% of South Australia with electricity. Commercial road is one of the main shopping areas and one of the oldest streets with several historic buildings and pubs. Watch out for signs with the route of the interpretive walk, photos and descriptions of the historic buildings.

More towns with unusual names were on the route – Bookaloo, (mostly a rest area) Tarcoola (once a goldfield) and Ooldea, a tiny settlement on the eastern edge of the Nullarbor Plain. It was the site of a mission for Aboriginal children. Ooldea was an important camp during construction of the Trans-Australian Railway, as it is near a permanent waterhole. The longest dead straight sector of the railway in the world starts west of Ooldea before Watson and continues to a point between Loongana and Nurina (more unusual names), a distance of 478 kilometres!

And now for the long haul to Perth, crossing some of the most God forsaken country you're ever likely to see. There are parts that resemble a moonscape. "The Nullarbor? You can't miss it", a steward tells a passenger. "It'll be outside all day". Ooondiri in the Aboriginal language means waterless. (Wanderlust, (2021, para. 2) states that...."Oondiri means waterless"). The horizon, engulfed in every direction, quantity, and almost perfectly flat, a pale green endlessness under dark skies. Hours and occasional acacia floated freely through the air. Apart from food , which was lip-smackingly good in Gold Kangaroo class, it was that no-nonsense approach to hospitality that seemed to impress my fellow passengers. "I reckon they're bloody marvellous, these Australians", said Bill, a Yorkshireman, over dinner one night. "Whenever I ask these young girls for something they say 'no worries' and it damn well gets done". Bill and his three travelling companions (all cricket enthusiasts who had left their wives back in England) quickly renamed the Indian Pacific the "No Worries Express". As Australia's parched interior rolled by – I slipped gradually, into the train's routine: eating, chatting, reading or staring out of the window. In the lounge, I quickly started conversations with retirees, insurance estimators, surgeons, graphic designers and retired bankers. A young forensic expert from Leeds – later offered a job in Queensland by one of the surgeons, said, "I'm off to Adelaide", I did think of flying from Sydney, but with three meals a day I reckon this is better value". And so it was. We dined on delicious soups, ingenious starters and a wide selection of main courses. Breakfasts were suitably hearty, with a choice of a full cooked menu, fresh fruit and porridge. "You know what impressed me?" said Joe, a retired college professor from New York – "It's the people. They have a confidence about themselves and are genuinely funny. Outside the cities, Australia is not so much funny as patently ludicrous – a country of dry, open spaces damaged extensively by the world's spiteful climate. Only those with significant optimism can survive in the remoter parts of the country. For anyone who really wants to get a feel for the immensity of the Australian landscape and the dramatic story of European settlement in this wide, brown land, a trip on the Indian Pacific is an absolute must. The Indian Pacific, like its sister train, the Ghan, provides more than just an encounter with the great Australian emptiness; such a journey reveals the energies that have shaped the national psyche – the optimism, humour and unexpected moments.

In 1917 the Trans-Continental railway was opened. There was no surveyed road west of Penong or east of Norseman until a dirt road was graded during the World War, still largely on the route taken by Edward John Eyre 100 years earlier. Finally the Eyre Highway was completely bitumen-sealed in 1976 after sections had been re-sited close to the Bight, with access to magnificent coastal scenery. You'll be greeted at sunrise by the striking raw beauty of the one of the largest plains in the world, on the journey of 1782 kilometres between Port Pirie and Kalgoorlie.

The name comes from the latin, nullus arbor, 'no trees'. A seemingly endless expanse of rusty earth and hardy outback shrubs, this vast arid plain of 200,000 square kilometres of South Australia and Western Australia, stretches inland from the Great Australian Bight which is rimmed by the longest length of unbroken cliff-line in the world, and contains no surface water, has sparse vegetation, and is almost uninhabited. It is considered a "bucket list" experience.

Among the towns that the Indian Pacific passed were Deakin, Forrest, Rawlinna (where there is a stop), Chifley, Curtin, Kalgoorlie (on the return journey, there is an excursion), Coolgardie, Southern Cross and Northam. There is much of interest along the track, the saltbush is typical of sheep station country and the Darwin road swings north to Kingoonya. We pass Tarcoola which began as a mining town and all along are relics of the battle fought to water the old steam stains in a vast area without a single stream. Beneath the Plain are limestone deposits up to 100 metres deep and these are honeycombed by many caves and large underground lakes and rivers.

Historically, the Nullarbor Plain was seasonally occupied by Indigenous peoples, the Spinifex and Wangai peoples.

The first Europeans known to have sighted and mapped the Nullarbor coast were Captain Francolis Thijssen, Councillor of the Indies, Pieter Nuyts, on the Gulden Zeepaert (the Golden Seahorse). In 1626-1627, they chartered a stretch of the southern Australian coast east of Cape Leeuwin. While the interior remained little known to Europeans over the next two centuries, the stretch of coast adjoining the Great Australian Bight was named for Nuyts, and maps subsequent to 1627 bore the legend "Landt van P. Nuyts" or "Terre de Nuyts".

Edward John Eyre became the first European to successfully cross the Nullarbor in 1841. Eyre departed Fowler's Bay on 17th November 1840 with John Baxter and a party of three Aboriginal men. When three of his horses died of dehydration, he returned to Fowler's Bay. He departed with a second expedition on 25th February 1841. By the 29th April the party had reached Caiguna. Lack of supplies and water led to mutiny, and two of the Aboriginal men killed Baxter and took the party's supplies. Eyre and the third Aboriginal man, Wylie, continued on their journey, surviving through bushcraft and by chance, received some supplies from a French whaling vessel anchored at Rossiter Bay. They completed their crossing in 1841.

During the British nuclear tests at Maralinga in the 1950's the government forced the Wangai to abandon their homeland. Since then they have been awarded compensation, and many have returned to the general area. Others never left.

In 2011 South Australian Premier Mike Rann announced that a huge area of the Nullarbor, stretching almost 200 kilometres from the Western Australian border to the Great Australian Bight, would be given formal Wilderness Protection Status. The area contains 390 species of plants and a large number of habitats for rare species of animals and birds. The Nullarbor Plain is a former shallow seabed. One theory is that the whole area was uplifted by crustal movements in the Miocene, and since then, erosion by wind and rain has reduced its thickness.

Most of the inhabited areas of the Nullarbor Plain can be found in a series of small settlements located along the railway, and in small settlements along the Eyre Highway that provide services to travellers, mostly spaced between one and two hundred kilometres apart. For many Australians, "Crossing the Nullarbor", is typically represented of a quality of experience of the "Australian Outback". Stickers bought from roadhouses on the highway show – "I have crossed the Nullarbor", can be seen on vehicles of varying capacity for long-distance travel. Over the years various runners and walkers have crossed the Nullarbor from west to east and visa versa, including the first non-Indigenous person Henri Gilbert, on foot! Thew!

We stopped at the ramshackled outpost of Cook which was once a thriving Nullarbor town with around 200 residents, its own hospital, school, golf course and shops. As remote towns go, it doesn't get any more isolated than this. The nearest town is 500 kilometres drive away! Today Cook is a ghost town (population 2), and someone has erected a sign for the Cook Golf Club – "New members welcome". Cook is in the western extreme of South Australia, in the harshest of climates, on the edge of the Nullarbor Plain, twice the size of England. With privatisation of the railways in 1997, the town was effectively closed and today has a permanent population of four, and serves as a refuelling station for the Indian Pacific and a stop-over for drivers. The use of highly durable concrete sleepers was adopted, and together with the ability of modern diesel locomotives to travel very long distances without refuelling, the number of staff needed dwindled. There is a sign titled 'The Middle of Nowhere' and reads "Welcome to Cook the Queen City of the Nullarbor, postcode 5710, population four. You are standing alongside the longest stretch of straight railway in the world, spanning 478 kilometres." The "main street", a dusty expanse between the railway and a line of unoccupied fibro homes, has a hand-painted sign warning "Cook – last fuel for 868 kilometres"; as if to say "venture beyond this point at your peril". According to Australian astronaut Andy Thomas, the rail line can even be spotted from space, looking like 'a very fine pencil line across the desert'. Another amusing sign reads "If you're crook, come to Cook, our hospital needs your help, get sick." It was a catchy phrase to try and get people to use the town's hospital, in order to prove its viability and existence. The settlement at Cook has two lonely lockups (goal,cells) but no policeman, but senior railway officials, however, have the power to make arrests. The goal cells, which are essentially two very small corrugated iron sheds that look more like outhouses than anything else. They were built to house criminals caught wandering on the Nullarbor and held there until the next train arrived; the two cells are matching "his" and "hers", complete with bars, padlocks and their own "goal house rock", serve as a photo opportunity for tourists. It comes as no surprise that few people use this route because if you get into trouble, you are very much on your own. On one of my occasions travelling on the Indian Pacific, we stopped to refuel. In the distance was seen a cloud of red dust coming towards us. A dusty van arrived, and out jumped its driver who threw open the van doors to reveal souvenirs, tea towels, keyrings etc. He quickly paraded up and down the length of the train plying his merchandise. What a character – I think he did good business that day!

Next was Deakin, which is the last railway siding in Western Australia on the Trans-Australian Railway. Deakin is important in the history of South Australia and Western Australia in the part it has played in the fixing of the Western Australian border with South Australia by marking the border on the ground. Forest, a small settlement and railway station on the railway in Western Australia, recorded that no people lived there. However 18 people were recorded in the 2006 census! Named after Sir John Forrest, the explorer who became the first Premier of Western Australia, Forrest is another town on the longest stretch of straight railway in the world. It has a typical arid climate: however cooler in summer than much of the Australian desert due to its proximity to the ocean. Temperatures of up to 50 degrees Celsius have been recorded here. Horrendous!

A popular disembarkation point for Jackaroos and Jillaroos, is Rawlinna, a railway siding which lies next to Australia's largest sheep station, 910 kilometres from Perth is the 2.5 million acre Rawlinna Station. Extablished in 1962, the station today stocks more than 80,000 sheep, with the wool regularly sent to Adelaide for testing and sale. In 2018 there were 64,000 sheep sheared for a wool clip of 1500 bales. Rawlinna has also a huge loop track, and some of the trains that head through the station here are 3km long. Rawlinna itself is also the site of the Loongana Lime Mine where the limestone extracted is mostly used in the gold production process at Kalgoorlie. We were treated to a special long-table dinner under the bright stars of the outback sky. Surrounded by nothing but vast sheep stations (the nearest town, Kalgoorlie, is more than 400 kilometres away). We disembarked to partake of drinks, and canapes served around a bonfire under the wide Nullarbor skies. This was one alfresco dining experience to remember.

I explored Rawlinna Station on another occasion (not enough time when you're on an off train excursion), via a four wheel drive vehicle. Whether you're into trainspotting, bird-watching or gazing at the stars, this trip is absolutely mesmerizing. Just after sunrise at Rawlinna I glimpsed the Indian Pacific's lights as it headed towards me from the west. The train had left Perth a day prior and travelled through the night. It slowly pulled into the station, a single blue and yellow locomotive with an eagle emblazoned on its front towing a kilometre of gleaming silver carriages. After a long delay, passengers came out; the two-hour morning tea stopover at Rawlinna is a regular schedule for eastbound passengers. Of course, the westbound passengers stop here for an evening meal under the stars. If you are here, it's a great opportunity to see the train pulled up in the middle of nowhere. In the days of high track maintenance Rawlinna had a regular population with a school, the remains of which are on the edge of town. There used to be gangs based there, but then the track's sleepers were changed from wood to concrete and regular maintenance wasn't required. Trains also became longer with greater range, so today the town is virtually deserted, except for a 'roo shooter' and some regular railway workers. However, the old post office and storefront looked like they could still open for business; they were built out of red brick and corrugated iron, and although the post office isn't manned, it's still possible to post a letter, as there's a box with the '6434' postcode. We followed the same route as the train in our four wheel drive vehicle and drove 375km along an unsealed road which passes by mines and then through tall woodlands, and there are glimpses of the railway along the way. It's a 'tyre killer' road covered with scrub and boulders and we left the road to bypass long sections of these stones. There are no services at Rawlinna, no shops nor accommodation, so you need to carry all necessities including fuel and water. The nights out here are magical; there's no glow from any external lights and you can see the headlights of the trains from many kilometres away.

We departed Rawlinna late that evening on the Indian Pacific, and at this point we were almost on the final stretch and all that lay ahead, was the thrust into Western Australia and the return of greener hues, towering trees and fields of cattle. It was so welcome after kilometres of red earth, as we made the final run towards the Indian Ocean. I found it all utterly fascinating, but I was curious to know what it was like for those who did the journey regularly? Train steward Joss, a man with a delightful curling moustache and a cheerful disposition, said "I never tire of it, no matter how often you do it, no two journeys on the Indian Pacific are ever the same. You always notice something different." We waited as long as we could, but by evening there was nothing for it but to declare officially that it was "beer o'clock" on the Indian Pacific. It was a little earlier than usual, but the circumstances were exceptional – and there was plenty to drink. As our arrival in Perth drew near, I asked many on board, "So when exactly is beer o'clock?" "Beer o'clock, it's whenever you feel like it."

CHAPTER 3

At Last Perth

On the third day we arrived at our destination, Perth. Such a beautiful city situated on the Swan River, known for the habitat of the black swan. I just had to see more of this city and stayed about a week before again boarding the Indian Pacific back to Sydney. As Australia's most remote capital city, Perth is home to over 1.9 million residents and serves as an important gateway to Asia.

Perth City is located in the ancient country of the Whadjuk Nyoongar people, who have been the traditional owners of the south west of Western Australia for at least 40,000 years. At the time of colonization in 1829, the Perth Nyoongar people were composed of four principal groups – Mooro, Beeliar, Beeloo, Weeip – loosely determined by the Swan River (or Derbari Yerrigan). "Country" is the term used by Aboriginal peoples to recognize, locate and connect unite themselves and each other to a particular language group and place (the land or sea) they identify with, belong to and have cultural commitments with. Colonization severely interrupted the Nyoongar people's society and economy – epidemic disease caused an immediate loss of life, and the occupation of land by settlers and the restriction of Aboriginal people to reserves disrupted their ability to support themselves.

Australia's sunniest capital city, Perth averages 3000 hours of sunshine per year and boasts 19 stunning beaches from the surf hub of Scarborough to the popular Cottesloe. It easily blends urban cool with raw natural beauty. Its heart is humming with new bars, restaurants, shopping and cultural spaces, and also home to Kings Park – one of the world's largest inner city parks. Just a short drive away are the beautiful beaches where you can watch amazing sunsets and even swim with wild dolphins. No wonder The New York Times declared Perth a 'hipster haven'.

If you're lucky enough to be in Perth in the Spring, you will see stunning wildflowers, amazing wildlife, and warm days. When the Indian Pacific arrived after its epic transcontinental crossing, I took a tour to explore the city. We were taken to Kings Park from where we had magnificent city views, travelled along the Swan River and picturesque foreshore parklands, saw Subiaco with its trendy boutiques and restaurants, and Claremont with its upmarket shopping and the famous 'Millionaire's Row'. We visited city landmarks like the WACA Cricket Ground, Town Hall, Perth Mint, Parliament House, Crown Casino and Barracks Arch. Barracks Arch was built to house the Enrolled Pensioner Force (also know as 'Pensioner Guards'). The guards who were retired military personnel came to Australia on the convict ships that transported nearly 10,000 prisoners to Western Australia between 1850-1868. They were given land grants and employment on arrival.

Kings Park is a 400.6-hectare park overlooking Perth's central business district. The park is a combination of grassed parkland, botanical gardens and natural bushland on Mount Eliza with two-thirds of the grounds conserved as native bushland. Offering panoramic views of the Swan River and Darling Range, it is home to over 324 native plant varieties, 25 known Indigenous fungi species and 80 bird species. This most popular tourist destination is visited by over five million people each year.

The Perth Mint is Australia's official bullion mint and wholly owned by the Western Australian Government. Established on 20th June 1899, the Perth Mint was the last of three Australian colonial branches of the United Kingdom's Royal Mint intended to refine gold from the gold rushes and to mint gold sovereigns and half-sovereigns for the British Empire. Perth has some of the most celebrated beaches in Australia.

Perth is the birthplace of many of Australia's best-loved beers such as Matilda Bay and Little Creatures and this tradition continues with several new openings such as the Northbridge Brewing Company, Mash Brewery and Feral

Brewing Company – plus a new-found obsession with arti-san gin, vodka and whisky.

Perth has some wonderful beaches and Scarborough Beach is the most famous beach for Perth residents. It has a very happening atmosphere and is always busy with many cafeterias around and plenty of options. Just 20 minutes from Perth CBD, it is one of the best beaches on the West Coast. A walk along the beach offers a view of a most strik-ing coastline and living here you can walk to many of other city beaches including the topless beach and a pet friendly beach. There are a myriad of restaurants and cafes as well as takeaway outlets. You can shop till you drop with an amaz-ing array of speciality and boutique stores (did someone say boutiques!), with in easy reach of the larger shopping centres of Perth. I'm in!

Cottesloe Beach is a popular beach and one of the most iconic locations of Western Australia. The continuing pop-ularity of the beach is the result of combination of factors including proximity to metropolitan Perth, accessibility by train, shelter from strong summer breezes and the presence of offshore reefs making it a relatively safe swimming location.

While you're in Perth, a visit to Fremantle is a must. It is 22.9 kilometres from Perth. Fremantle is a port city in Western Australia, located at the mouth of the Swan River in the metropolitan area of Perth the state capital. The Western Australian vernacular diminutive for Fremantle is Freo. Prior to British settlement, the Indigenous Noongar people inhabited the area for millennia, and knew it by the name of Walyalup (place of the Woylie-a small kangaroo-like marsu-pial with a long tail that has a black brush at the end). Visited by Dutch explorers in the 1600s, Fremantle was the first area settled by the Swan River colonists in 1829, and is named after Captain Charles Fremantle, an English naval officer who claimed the west coast of New Holland (as Australia was called then) as British territory. Fremantle became Australia's primary destination for convicts. Fremantle Prison which is now a World Heritage site, operated long after transportation ended in 1868, It became a bustling trade centre and gateway at the height of the Western Australian gold rushes. It was declared a city in 1929 and was a destination for migrants particularly from Italy after World War 11.

Not far from Perth (132 kms) is the only monastic town in Australia. It is situated next to the banks of the Moore River. On March 1 1846, a Benedictine mission to the local native Aborigines was started about 8 kms to the north, led by the two Spanish Benedictine monks, Rosendo Salvado and Joseph Serra. There are so many experiences to be had at New Norcia - magnificent architecture, the cultural and historic heritage, the art galleries and museum. You can join a spiritual retreat and take in the serenity of the bushland setting and taste the delicious New Norcia food. I joined a guided tour around the town visiting among other things, the Abbey which was founded by Benedictine Rudesindus Salvado. There are currently 7 monks who pray together seven times a day living in the monastery. The history of New Norcia is fascinating. In 1835 the government of Spain dissolved all religious communities in the country. Among those who were exiled were Dom Rosendo Salvado and Dom Joseph Serra who had been Benedictine monks in Compostela. They both applied for foreign missions and were attached to the newly appointed Bishop of Perth, Dr. John Brady. In February 1846, Salvado and Serra, accompanied by a French monk Tootel and an Irish catechist set out towards a farmhouse which was located 130 kilometres north of Perth. Shortly after their arrival in the area they established their mission for the local Aborigines beside a spring 8 kilometes north of the present site of New Norcia. The early settlement was fraught with catastrophes. The order ran out of money, Dom Tootel returned to England, the Aborigines plundered the settlement, life was unbelievably hard, and there seemed to very little success in converting the local inhabitants to Christianity. In 1847 the settlement was moved to the banks of the Moore River and named New Norcia, after Norcia, Italy, the birthplace of the order's founder, St Benedict. By 1848 the mission had more than 1000 acres of land and both sheep and cattle were being grazed. A decade later the mission was separated from the control of Perth. The mission grew in significance in the 1860s and 1870s as the monks established a series of wells in the area and horses were bred and silk produced. In 1867 it became an Abbey and the remarkable Dom Rosendo Salvado, who by this time had learnt the language of the local people. You can taste some of the delicious New Norcia produce, freshly baked New Norcia bread, silver medal winning olive oil, grown in the 100 year old Monastery olive grove and palatable wines and ports from the Abbey wines label. That was a most interesting and informative place.

When it's time to relax and refresh, swap the rush of the city for an idyllic island escape with a contrast at Rottnest Island. Rottnest Island, known colloquially as Rotto, is off the coast located 18 kilometres west of Fremantle and covers 19 square kilometres and is a popular destination for tourists. I travelled over by boat, and stayed overnight at the Ocean View units situated close to the ocean, with a view over the tranquil waters from my balcony. It is easily reached by a short ferry ride from the mainland and is car-free, so I hired a bicycle when I arrived. Rottnest is well know for its population of quokkas, a small native marsupial found in very few other locations. I met other tourists at the Rottnest Volunteer Guides information booth and took a guided walk around the settlement to learn about the life of the Quokkas. I had seen their charming faces in magazines, but I didn't know that Quokkas love a good riddle and make incredible detectives. The Quokka is as curious as it is adorable, so it's very likely they'll come up to YOU. With camera ready be respectful and keep your distance so they feel confidant enough to let you seize this special meeting. The island is also home to colonies of Australian Sea Lions and Southern Fur Seals. The island prides itself in having 63 beaches and 20 bays and you'll be spoilt for choice with pure white sand beaches and clear blue waters in all manner of ways, which makes it a beach-lovers paradise. Sea Kayak, Rottnest's glass bottom kayak company gives you a window into the water below where you'll spot all kinds of colourful coral and marine life. Both airport and the main ferry landing are located on the eastern side of the island. Human artefacts have been found on the island dating back at least 30,000 years and the island is called Wadjemup (place across the water where the spirits are) by the Noongar people. Rottnest Island (Wadjemup in the local Aboriginal language, holds a special significance for the local Noongar people. I joined a group on an absorbing walking tour with a Noongar guide who gave us a unique meaning, culture and history from his perspective. The island was named by Willem de Vlamingh in 1696, he called it Rottenest (Rat's Nest Island) after the quokka population.

It was back to Perth's East Terminal to again board the great Indian Pacific for the 4352 kilometre journey home to Sydney where I would prepare for my next rail odyssey. The journey from the Indian Ocean to the Pacific Ocean began as the bold wedge-tailed eagle emblemed train pulled away from the platform in Perth mid-morning. The wedge-tailed eagle emblem symbolises the scope, range and significance of each epic journey the Indian Pacific traverses - mountain ranges, arid deserts, goldfields, rocky valleys and subtropical savannahs on its transcontinental crossings. I think there's no better way to experience the spectacular interior landscape of Australia than by the romance of rail.

CHAPTER 4

Home to Sydney

I settled into my comfortable cabin and again got to know the familiar creature comforts of life onboard. As we glided through the picturesque rolling hills of the Avon Valley, we were served a modern Australian lunch, and after enjoyed a relaxing afternoon onboard, to be followed by a three-course dinner prior to our late evening arrival in Kalgoorlie, where the Indian Pacific pauses again after the mind-numbing vastness of the Nullarbor. If I hadn't been careful about limiting my intake of those delicious meals, I would've ended up looking like the back of the Indian Pacific! There was an excursion out to a mine but it was too dark to properly see anything, so I stayed in the train's lounge and chatted with the other passengers.

I stayed in Kalgoorlie on a trip some years ago. Kalgoorlie is where gold was discovered very early during European settlement. In 1893 Paddy Hannan discovered gold on the west-

ern fringes of the Nullarbor Plain, and shortly after prospectors and prostitutes descended into town in search of fortune,
and the rest is history. This find probably made Australia, or
certainly kicked it off to a great start. Kalgoorlie-Boulder is
home to the staggering 3.6 kilometre wide Fimiston Open
Pit known as the Super Pit, (so big it can be seen from space)
an open-cut gold mine which has operated 24 hours a day
since 1989. It was Australia's largest open cut gold mine until
it was surpassed by the Newmont Boddington gold mine also
in Western Australia. From the safety of a bus I toured the
Super Pit. I was amazed by the size of the 793 dump trucks
as we travelled along the haul roads on site with the trucks.
The view of the Super Pit from Harvey Hut nearly blew me
away as I saw the old miner's workings with old shafts and
viewed the modern mining machinery working in the pit. At
the internal lookout, passengers were able to get out of the
bus and view the operation from a different viewpoint than
that at the Super Pit lookout.

Kalgoorlie-Boulder, as it is more commonly known, is
the heart of the Western Australian Goldfields and the largest
city in the Australian outback. From tempestuous origins as
a gold rush town full of fortune-seekers, it has grown into a
lively twin city with an idiosyncratic character. Hay Street
was a notorious red light area for most of the history of
Kalgoorlie. The presence of brothels was part of the law and
order issue of an isolated mining town, where two-up, pros-
titution and gold stealing were all regularly reported forms of
criminality. The area gained a reputation for being the "Wild
West". The strip was lined with dozens of brothels. However
there is now only one brothel left in Kalgoorlie, the Red
House. In the latest development, the Red House has closed
as a working brothel. Sign of the times. Kalgoorlie remains
one of the most important mining areas in the world, with

several large mining operations located in and around the city, including the Super Pit.

As rich in history as it is in gold, the city has an impressive array of heritage buildings, including the magnificent Kalgoorlie and Boulder Town Halls, as well as grand hotels, outback pubs, shop fronts and private homes. A visit to the Goldfields War Museum and the Museum of the Goldfields will also offer a fascinating insight into the area's colourful past. Beyond the city, spooky ghost towns tell the story of early gold prospecting dreams that have long been abandoned.

The Aboriginal history and culture of Western Australia's Golden Outback were shaped by the ancient tribes that have inhabited the region for many thousands of years. These include the Wongi people of the Western Desert and the Goldfields, the Yamatji people of the Gascoyne-Murchison region and the Noongar people from the Wheatbelt and Esperance-South Coast. The basis of Indigenous culture and spiritual beliefs is the Dreaming. The ancestral Dreaming spirits, who could change their form into animals, people or any physical feature, travelled across the country shaping the natural environment and establishing religious and moral systems for Indigenous Australians. You can explore the Indigenous history and culture of Western Australia's Golden Outback by joining one of the many authentic Indigenous tours.

The Indian Pacific passed Coolgardie which first made world headlines when gold was discovered there in 1892. It became known as the birthplace of the gold rush that inspired mass migration of people in Australia's history. I was surprised to learn that the town was once home to over 16,000 residents, with two stock exchanges, three breweries, seven newspapers and 26 hotels. If you take a walk down the wide main street, you'll see grand glimpses of its glory days. Many of these heritage buildings remain today, including the Mining Warden's Court that houses the Goldfields and

Coolgardie Museum – a great introduction to the Goldfield's vivid early social history. If you want to spend a day nearer to nature beyond the town, the fresh water wetlands of Rowles Lagoon offers swimming, boating, canoeing, bush walking, bird watching, picnic spots and the opportunity to camp under a star-filled outback night sky.

We arrived in Cook South Australia in the afternoon, and as I had been to Cook on the way over, I got off and wandered around until it was time to depart. We journeyed on our way to Adelaide and along the way the tremendous beauty of the country manifested itself. An early arrival in Adelaide allowed us several excursions, having been on most of them, I took a city tour.

We departed at 3.20pm and travelled overnight on our way to Broken Hill. We arrived in the afternoon, time for an excursion. For my excursion, this time I chose the visit to the Palace Hotel which was featured in the movie Priscilla Queen of the Desert, to see the drag show. There's a lot of involvement from the audience and it was heaps of fun. I was there during the 'Heels Festival' mostly held at the Palace and it was a laugh from beginning to the end. Concerts were held both outdoors and indoors at the hotel with lots of Drag Queens strutting their stuff. The hotel commemorates Priscilla with murals in the foyer and memorabilia, definitely worth seeing. There was no time for me to see the other concerts, being on an off train excursion, however, I booked for the following year's 3 day festival.

Broken Hill which is famous for the discovery of silver, has inspired an array of artists over the years with its distinctive desert landscape. You can visit the late Pro Hart gallery, where you'll learn all about one of Australia's most celebrated artists, whose works, known all over the world, captures the spirit of the area. This gallery is worth a visit and there is a shop where you can purchase paintings and souvenirs. Most paintings are inspired by and set in the vastness of the Australian Outback.

Aboriginal people have lived in the area for at least 45,000 years and traditionally there are more than 38 Aboriginal language groups. Movie buffs will delight in spotting the settings featured in many movies produced here, including Mad Max, Priscilla Queen of the Desert, Dirty Deeds and Race the Sun.

While you are there you can take in the giant Big Picture canvas diorama of the outback. You'll be delighted by Broken Hill's much admired attraction. It's the world's largest acrylic painting by a single artist housed in the Silver City mint and Art Centre. Ando, a Broken Hill local artist completed the 12m x 100m canvas over a two-year period which features a striking scene of lightning strikes, dust storms, mountains and a saltbush landscape. Not able to be expressed in words, the painting is an immersive experience of walking into a painting. You will hear more about the history behind the "Big Picture" as you enjoy drinks and canapes served on the deck area.

Named by the explorer Charles Sturt who described the nearby Barrier Range as a "broken hill" in his account of the area. It is home to the world's richest lead-zinc ore deposit. If it's epic Australian scenery you're after, look no further than Broken Hill, where you can see the vast desert scapes of Mundi Mundi and the breathtaking colourful and rugged scenery of the desert from the lookout. I found this to be one of the most remarkable panoramas that I had ever seen.

While Broken Hill's history is synonymous with mining, the Bulali and the Wilyakali people inhabited this area for millennia before any mineral wealth was unlocked. The Wilyakali called the region home for 50,000 years or more. In this part of Australia, you can see plenty of evidence of one of the oldest living civilisations on earth, such as the brilliant collection of Aboriginal rock art at Mutawintji to the north-east of the city.

Broken Hill was a stronghold of unionism and organized labour. Strikes were prevalent, notably in the early 1900s. The biggest industrial dispute, known as the "Great Strike", lasted 18 months between May 1919 and November 1920, involving thousands of mine workers. It secured proper recognition of the rights and conditions of working in the mining industry and was the foundation for many of the rights we take for granted today, including a 35-hour week, workplace safety and compensation.

The city also lays claim to being the only site of an enemy attack on Australian soil in WW1. In 1915, two Turkish patriots raised a Turkish flag over their ice-cream cart and opened fire on passengers aboard the Silverton Tramway Company's train, which was heading to an annual picnic. Two years prior in 1913, a monument to the Titanic's musicians was erected in Sturt Park. Instigated by the bandsmen of Broken Hill, it stands nearly six metres high and carries the names of all the ship's musicians who drowned. During WW11, vast quantities of the nation's gold reserves were stored at Broken Hill, because of the ever-present fear of Japanese invasion. The government decided that gold was safer inland. It was removed from the vaults of the Commonwealth Bank in various capital cities and stored in a purpose-built strongroom at the Broken Hill goal.

Two legendary Outback bases can be found there – the Royal Flying Doctor Service and the School of the Air. Australia is a big place, 7.69 million square kilometres big, and with a relatively small population of about 25 Million people.

The Royal Flying Doctor Service provides medical service to a third of the population which lives across rural and remote areas- sometimes more than a 6 hour drive to the closest township. Medical services that are taken for granted in cities are for the most part not possible outside metropolitan areas. It amounts to real hardships for the families and communities living in the "bush." The Royal Flying Doctor provides 24 hour aeromedical emergency services to country Australia. Accidents, injuries, heart attacks, can generally be reached anywhere with a 2 hour period. Recently the RFDS has brought mental health and therapeutic services to Broken Hill and surrounding towns. "The Wellbeing Place" as it is called, provides an opportunity to expand their range of services from clinical treatment to workshops and programs for welfare which includes yoga and meditation.

The Royal Flying Doctor Service was founded by the Reverend John Flynn who was born in Moliagul, central Victoria on 25 November, 1880. Graduating from secondary school in 1898 John began school teaching. In 1903 he joined the ministry and studied theology at Ormond College, at the University of Melbourne. Initially he financed his studies working at Church Home Ministry Centres around Victoria, and in 1907 commenced a four year course in divinity at Melbourne University. He was ordained as a Minister of the Presbyterian Church in 1911. Throughout his training John continued to develop an interest in working in the Outback and in early 1911 John was on the road to the real Outback. For the next ten years, Flynn campaigned for an aerial medical service. His vision was to provide a "mantle of safety" for the people of the bush, and the vision became a reality when his long time supporter, H.V. McKay left a large bequest for "an aerial experiment" which enabled Flynn to get the Flying Doctor Service airborne. The first pilot, Arthur Affleck, had no navigational aids, no radio and only a compass. He navigated by landmarks such as fences, rivers, river beds, dirt roads or just wheel tracks and telegraph lines. In its inaugural year, the Aerial Medical Service (which changed its name to the Royal Flying Doctor Service in 1955) flew 50 flights to

26 destinations and treated 225 patients. Flynn's dream had become a reality. The Australian Council Office collaborated with the Reserve Bank of Australia in 1994 on the design of the twenty dollar note, which features the face of the founder of the Royal Flying Doctor Service of Australia, the Very Reverend John Flynn. He once said "if you start something worthwhile – nothing can stop it" and this simple truth is evidenced by the RFDS today, over 90 years on (Royal Flying Doctor Service (ND. para. 22).

The other legendary Outback base is the School of the Air which is a Distance Education Centre. It was established in 1956 and now caters predominantly for the geographically isolated students within a radius of approximately 300k from Broken Hill. The school aims to develop excellence in learning over distance through open communication and personalized teacher/pupil and home supervisor interaction. Our excursion that day took us behind the scenes at the school and there we saw a lesson in action, and met the teachers. The students of course are supervised at home and it was once all done via a peddle radio. These days lessons are conducted largely over the internet, with satellite link-ups allowing the 130 pupils to interact with each other and their teacher. Instead of classrooms, there are studios. Each contains a bank of technology more suited to Google's HQ or NASA control centre. It is a true marvel of modern communications.

I had never ridden a camel before, and on another occasion when I re-visited Broken Hill, I joined a group being taken on a ride. The cameleer who could sell sand to the Egyptians, talked us into a 2 ½ hour sunset tour. I was amazed at how comfortable they were, such a strange feeling. We had the good fortune to have the best sunset I had ever seen. Whilst stopped to admire the serenity and sunset a couple of emus just sauntered passed the half dozed kangaroos grazing – all this within 20 metres from our little group.

There was something extraordinary about what we were saw and experiencing. The serenity of this whole experience was "mind boggling" and naturally there were bush yarns from the cameleer.

If you're in Broken Hill on an occasion when there's time for an excursion, you'll do well to visit Silverton, the historic one pub mining town on the edge of the desert west of Broken Hill. If it wasn't for the small community of artists, its desirability as a setting for outback movies, there would never have been this never ending tourist trade. Located close to the South Australian border, this once thriving mining town (at one point it had a population of 3,000) is now nothing more than a few historic buildings, the remnants of once-vibrant streets, several art galleries and a pub. When visiting the town, travel a few kilometres to the Mundi Mundi lookout, and you can gaze at the horizon over barren desert, have a drink at the pub and visit the Day Dream Mine, the last mine that is still open for inspection. The Silverton Public School, which evolved into a Museum, was where its most famous teacher, Mary Jane Cameron became the famous Australian poet, Dame Mary Gilmore. The Museum houses photographs and artefacts which tell the stories of the district and of education in outback Australia. The Silverton Hotel used to have a token white horse outside to offer photographic opportunities and attract tourists. The horse would front up and wait until the publican gave it an ice cream – this scenario was repeated daily. Then came the movie boom, spearheaded by Wake in Fright in 1970. The horse was replaced by the Mad Max 2 car. It has been used in films as diverse as Wake in Fright, Mad Max 2 (there's a Museum celebrating this movie), Hostage, Razorback, Journey into Darkness, Dirty Deeds, The Craic and Golden Soak. This is a pub with character and a sardonic sense of humour typical of outback Australia. The Day Dream Mine, where one can experience a genuine "mining experience", is located about 3 km out of Silverton. Apart from the old mine, the area has evidence of its mining heyday with bits of machinery, boilers and other equipment littering the site.

Prior to the arrival of Europeans, the Wiljali Aborigines, who were desert people, moved through this area of unreliable water supplies. They called the region home for 50,000 years or more. You can see, in this part of Australia evidence of one of the oldest living civilisations on earth, such as the brilliant collection of Aboriginal rock art at Mutawintji to the north-east of the town. They were decimated by European disease and forcibly driven from the lands which underscored their self-sufficiency and their entire culture. More recently the Paarkinji (sometimes written Barkinji) have moved into the area from the lower Darling river.

Not far from Broken Hill is the small town of Menindee, the first town to be established on the Darling River. The Menindee district lies within the traditional lands of the Barkindji people who occupied the area for at least 35,000 years before the arrival of Europeans. The Barkindji or the Paakantyi people, today derive from several dialects, all speaking variations of the same language or Barlku. The land was harsh: drought was not rare and when the parched conditions set in, the Barkindji would withdraw into the backcountry around the few perennial springs, and cull the starving wildlife that came to refresh themselves there. In Barkindji lore, the landscape of and around the river was created by Ngatji, the dreamtime rainbow serpent, who is still believed to travel underground from waterhole to waterhole, and should not be disturbed. His presence is seen in such phenomena as when whirly breezes stir up the Darling's waterways. Aboriginal people became increasingly concentrated along the Darling River as the nearby Willandra Lakes system began to dry out after the last ice age 20,000 years ago. Famous as the last stop for ill-fated explorers Burke and Wills, the tiny town of Menindee is the oldest European settlement in Western NSW and the first town to be established on the Darling River. Once an important hub in the 1800s, Menindee now draws visitors to its stunning inland lakes and natural wonders. Menindee was founded in the 1850s and the first business to open its doors was the Menindee Hotel, now known as the Maiden's Hotel. For the first time in five years Menindee Lakes are brimming with water. Following thousands of years of Aboriginal habitation, the Menindee Lakes and the Darling River became a lifeline for early European explorers in one of the world's most arid regions.

It was time for the journey home to Sydney. Next stop, Mt. Victoria in the Blue Mountains. The Blue Mountains is made up of one million hectares of tall forests, sandstone cliffs, canyons and waterfalls. I was charmed by the blue horizon of eucalyptus trees that appeared to stretch on forever. One can explore on foot 140 kilometres of walking tracks and listen to Dreaming stories told by local Aboriginal guides. It's best to join a guided tour which among other things, offers a rich Aboriginal walking tour with a local Darug guide. You can ride the world's steepest passenger railway, the Scenic Railway. Passengers choose their level of adventure, adjusting their seated position up to 20 degrees. Choose Cliffhanger at a steep 64 degrees incline, Laidback for a more relaxed journey, or for loyal fans, Original at 52 degrees. To get the best views of World Heritage landscapes one must ride the Scenic Skyway. This 720 metre journey provides the ultimate views of Katoomba Falls, the Three Sisters, Mt. Solitary and the Jamison Valley. When the explorers Blaxland, Lawson and Wentworth crossed the Blue Mountains in 1813, in search for more grazing land for the young Sydney colony, they discovered what Australia's Aboriginal people had known for millennia: it's a big, beautiful country out there. There was an excursion after breakfast via coach to Scenic World , and passengers would then travel to Sydney by suburban train. Having been to the Blue Mountains on other occasions, I chose to travel back on the Indian Pacific.

At last, when Sydney Central station come into sight, I knew I was home. Wrapped around one of the world's greatest harbours, Sydney serves its natural wonders with an impressive array of worldly accomplishments, including a dynamic fusion-food scene spawned from the city's rich cultural mix, and not to mention the Olympics in 2000.

On 19th April 1770, the crew of HMS Endeavour, commanded by Lieutenant (later Captain) James Cook, were the first known Europeans to sight the east coast of Australia. Later they moored off a low headland boarded by sand dunes. Cook named the inlet Botany bay in honour of botanist Sir Joseph Banks who was impressed by the volume of flora and fauna.

The arrival of Lt James Cook marked the beginning of the end for the ancient way of life for the Aboriginal people. The original Aboriginal inhabitants of Sydney City local area are the Gadigal people. Their territory stretched along the southern side of Port Jackson (Sydney Harbour) from South Head to around what is now known as Petersham. The southern boundary is the area that now forms the Alexandra canal and Cooks river. Referred to collectively as the Eora Nation, the 29 clan groups of the Sydney metropolitan area have always lived in Sydney. Aboriginal communities here were both generous and combative towards the colonisers, and many places around the harbour remained important hunting, fishing and camping grounds long after European settlement and continue to be culturally significant today. Since European settlement in 1788, the Aboriginal people have been afflicted by an unnatural world for thousands of years. The arrival of the strangers who carried with them diseases, decimated the population of the Sydney tribes. The colonists were led to believe that the land was terra nullius (no one's land), which Lt James Cook declared Australia to be in 1770 during his first voyage around the coast. "...they were so ignorant they thought there was only one race on the earth and that was the white race". So when Captain Cook first set foot on Wangal land over at Kundul which is now called Kurnerll, he said "oh lets put a flag up somewhere, because these people are illiterate, they've got no fences". "They didn't understand that we didn't need fences....that we stayed here for six to eight weeks, then moved somewhere else where there was plenty of tucker and bush medicine and we kept moving and then come back in twelve month's time when the food was all refreshed...(Aboriginal Heritage Office (2008, para. 2) states that..."They didn't understand that we didn't fences...)". Quote - The late Aunty Beryl Timbery Beller. The Late Auntie Beryl Timbery Beller Came to Sydney from Walgett 50 Years ago to work as a nanny for an affluent white family. She said that her people were realizing that they also had to own their own businesses. She came from the Gamilaraay people of north-west NSW, and dreamed of opening a mostly Aboriginal-owned café, and did so in the 1980's. Aunty Beryl, as she liked to be known, wanted the café to introduce people to the delights of foods like lemon myrtle aioli, wattle seed pancakes and kangaroo pie. She used the café to give young Aboriginal and Torres Strait Islander hospitality students a chance to hone their knives and develop their culinary skills. The café has been closed since March, 2020. It was housed in the Gothic-style lodge built by Edmund Blacket in 1885, in Victoria Park. It was originally the home of the University of Sydney's groundskeepers, who tended the beautiful lawns surrounding the campus. The park was special because there was a lot of Aboriginal history. "We're overlooking a waterhole there and that was an Aboriginal meeting place. It was also a gathering place for the animals and the birds, and there was some bush tucker there". Quote: The Late Auntie Beryl Timbery Beller. Over the years the students she had taught at the Yaama Dhiyaan Hospitality Training College in Darlington have gone on to work as waiters, housemaids, concierges, chefs and baristas.

The early Europeans lacked an understanding of the Aboriginal way of life when first they came upon it. This excerpt taken from the diary of Watkin Tench, an officer in the First Fleet:

> "It does not appear that these poor creatures have any fixed habitation; sometimes sleeping in a Cavern of Rock, which they make as warm as an oven by lighting a fire in the middle of it, they will take up their abode here, for one night perhaps, then in another the next night. At other times (and we believe mostly in summer) they take up their lodgings for a day or two in a miserable Wigwam, which they made from bark of a tree. There are

dispersed about the woods near the water, 2, 3, 4 together; some oyster, cockle and muscle shells lie about the entrance of them, but not any quantity to indicate they make these huts their constant habitation. We met with some that seemed entirely deserted indeed it seems pretty evident that their habitation, whether caverns or Wigwams, are common to all, and alternatively inhabited by different tribes" (Tench, Watkins, (1788, para. 7), states that...."It does not appear that these poor creatures have any fixed habitation...").

For Aboriginal people and, in this instance, the clans living on the northern shores of Sydney, nothing could have been further from the truth. What the early colonists assumed , and perhaps what many Australians are only now beginning to understand, was that the Aboriginal lifestyle was based on common origin with the natural environment. Knowledge and understanding obtained over thousands of years, enabled them to use their environment to the maximum. For Aboriginal people, killing animals for food or building a shelter were steeped in ritual and spirituality, and carried out in perfect harmony with their surroundings.

"....from time immemorial, we believe as Aboriginal people, Australia has been here from the first sunrise, our people have been here along with the continent, with the first sunrise. We know our land was given to us by Baiami, we have a sacred duty to protect that land, we have a sacred duty to protect all the animals that we have an affiliation with through our totem system" (Munro,

Jenny, (ND. para. 6) states that… "from timer immemorial, we believe as Aboriginal people, Australia has been here from the first sunrise….)". Jenny Munro, Wiradjuri nation.

European civilization devastated people who have existed since before the time of legal memory. Because the vast majority of clans living in the Sydney basin were killed as a result of the 1788 intrusion, the stories of the land have been lost forever. There was no first hand witness accounts giving the Aboriginal people a proper and accurate point of view to what was happening. Aboriginal history has been handed down by ways of stories, dances, myths and legends.

After World War 11, the first wave of migration began with Displaced Persons. They fled their country of origin which had been destroyed by war or overrun by invaders. The second wave of post-war immigration arrived in the 1950's and 1960's, and consisted of those seeking employment and better living conditions. Between 1945 and 1965 more than two million migrants came to Australia. Many eventually settled in Sydney after spending time in hostels. Some found work on the Snowy Mountains Hydro Electric Scheme, others in factories, and heavy industry.

Today Chinese immigrants are the third largest group of migrants to come to Sydney (the immigration of which dates back to two hundred years) after United Kingdom and New Zealand. Sydney is probably one of the most multicultural cities of the world. It is home to me and over 5,000,000 other people.

CHAPTER 5

Sydney Central
Railway Station

The heritage listed Sydney Central Railway Station, opened on 4th August, 1906, is the oldest railway station in Australia. It is the main terminal in Australia for interstate as well as the Sydney local railway, and is located in the heart of the city. It offers connectivity to Sydney Airport, the Blue Mountains, and the light rail starts here as well.

Next time you board a train at Sydney Central Station, take a moment to think about the people that have lived around there, and the places that have been there for ages.

The original inhabitants of the local area are the Gadigal people who lived there for thousands of years. Following the arrival of Europeans, Aboriginal people have been forced into a world unnatural to their traditional culture which has existed for thousands of years. Europeans carried with them diseases which devastated the immediate population of the Sydney tribes. Prince Alfred Park next to Central Railway Station, was a campsite for Aboriginal peoples during the early 19th century. Also known as Cleveland Paddocks, this site was home to a large part of Sydney's Aboriginal population as they fled their land around Sydney Cove due to the violence and deprivation caused by European colonization. But despite the destructive impact of first contact, Gadigal culture survived, and as Sydney developed into a city, the Gadigal were joined by other Aboriginal people from around NSW to live, work and forge relationships with the urban Aboriginal community.

When you wake up to the possibility of searching Sydney's unsung histories, you realize places have been taken for granted, like Central Station, can be rich locales of revelations. In so doing you can better understand Sydney's past, and how you might portray it as home to over 5,000,000 people, in the future.

It is a very busy station, but I found that the polite and friendly staff will go out of their way to assist you. The main building's Grand Concourse, amazing by itself, compliments the rest of the architecturally photogenic building. Situated on the Grand Concourse are a number of eateries including the Eternity Café where you can have hot meals accompanied by wines when you step off the train. There is also a wonderful memorial to the railway staff who fell during the Great War. Upgrading programs were undertaken in 1955 and again in 1964.

In 1955 a booking hall was constructed. Murals illustrating railway scenes lined the walls, and a beautiful terrazzo map of Australia was created on the floor. The main features of the hall were designed by the renowned Italian artisans the Melocco brothers who migrated here, and built by Guido Zuliani, an artist they brought out from Italy. The mural was covered in greasy film and left to decompose above a food court and damaged by smoke from a kitchen fire, but now a celebrated mural portraying train travel in New South Wales has been brought back to life. A small team of conservation experts spent a month at Central Station lovingly rejuvenating the large design, which was made from a fine plaster and polished to look like marble. Julian Bickersteth from International Conservation Services and his team were brought in by Sydney Trains to clean up and detail the surface. Sydney Trains heritage specialist Gretta Logue said she thought the mural was destroyed in the fire as she watched the flames on the TV news. Now that the surface has been cleaned up and detailed, people can clearly see a story unfold. The railways understood the land they were travelling over, so an Indigenous motif takes pride of place.

The Eternity Cafè, so named to honour Arthur Malcolm Stace (1885 – 1967), who, would write the word "Eternity" on pavements all over Sydney. Born in an underprivileged family, Stace said he became a ward of the state when he was 12 years old. He claimed he was gaoled for drunkenness, lost a string of jobs and turned to stealing. He worked on and off as a booze courier from a hotel in Surry Hills, making deliveries to "two-up" schools (see note at the end of the chapter) and houses of ill-fame. He enlisted in the Australian Imperial Force on 18th March, 1916, and having served as a private with the 19th Battalion in France, probably as a drummer and stretcher-bearer, and at A.I.F. headquarters in England, he returned to Australia in February 1919 and was discharged medically unfit on 2nd May. He fell back into his old ways, drunk, broke and out of work.

In August 1930 Stace was motivated by a preacher at Pyrmont to give up the 'grog'. He helped impoverished men at R.B.S. Hammond's hostel, conducted open-air meetings in the city and he visited the Francis Street Methodist hostel, Callan Park Mental Hospital and the Lazaret. The Lazaret was erected in 1890 and was established as a hospital for infectious diseases. On the 22nd January 1942 he married Ellen Esther (Pearl) Dawson, at St. Barnabas's Anglican Church Sydney, and said of himself, I am a 'missioner'.

After being inspired by the evangelist John Ridley, who told a congregation in the Burton Baptist Tabernacle, that he wished he could 'shout eternity through the streets of Sydney', Stace felt a powerful call from the Lord to write "Eternity" on pavements. He tried writing 'Obey God', but the one word message of "Eternity" he said, made people think.

The Battle of Central Station

The station enjoyed a somewhat undisturbed existence, but in 1916 a little known riot took place dubbed the Battle of Central Station (was also known as the Liverpool Riot 1916). Soldiers stationed at Casula near Liverpool were asked to put in an hour and a half's extra work each day, meaning that in some cases men were asked to do 27 hours' work without a break. The word quickly spread, and from about 10 am on the 15th February, soldiers opposing the harsh camp conditions, started to invade the Liverpool railway station. A large and noisy crowd stormed hotels in Liverpool, drank them dry, damaged buildings, commandeered trains, and travelled to the city. The supplies of several hotels and other local businesses were ransacked. An hour later the first train reached Central station where they ran amok uncontrolled, destroying the station's facilities, and gun fire was exchanged between them and the military police. One rebel was shot dead and several were injured. Most of the violence took place at Central, and soldiers also ran through the streets damaging buildings and clashing with armed military guards.

Soldiers rioted for fourteen hours; about 15,000 soldiers took part in the revolt. In an effort to regain control, the military authorities ordered all soldiers to parade at 11am on 15th February at the Liverpool camp. The majority of soldiers managed to get back to camp and there were only 206 men absent of the estimated 3000 soldiers who marched up George Street in the city. Anyone who was not on parade was charged with desertion. In the following weeks, at least 279 soldiers were discharged from the Australian Imperial Force (AIF) for misconduct, drunkenness and being absent without leave or desertion. One soldier, Private William Roy Heaton was charged with "maliciously breaking a plate glass window at the Grace Bros department store worth £10" at the Sydney Quarter Sessions. Heaton, who was from Newcastle, was found guilty and sentenced to six months with hard labour. There was a public wave of sympathy for Heaton, supported by "The Mirror of Australia" newspaper. He was only sixteen, an orphan, and provided financial support for his younger sister. Heaton served his time at Goulburn goal and although he was originally sentenced to six months, he served about ten weeks. He was released on 28th March 1916 by special licence. He wrote to The Mirror:

"Dear Mr. Editor, I am not much of a scholar, so you must not mind if this letter is short. I have to thank The Mirror for taking up my case, and securing my release, and I hope now that I shall be allowed to re-join the Light Horse Brigade and get to the Front. That is where I want to be, with the boys in the trenches". (NSW Government State Archives & Records 2016).

Heaton was discharged with dishonour from the AIF upon his release from goal. On the 30th June 1916, he re-enlisted under another name, William Westacott. He served with the 35th Battalion and did not reveal his true identity until 5 February 1918.

Since Australia had a shortage of troops, the government discouraged media from covering the incident to avoid damage to the image of the Australian digger. Many escaped punishment, only about 1000 soldiers were court martialled, some gaoled and others discharged. This incident had a direct influence on the introduction of 6 o'clock closing of hotels in 1916, which lasted in New South Wales until 1955.

The evidence of the gun battle is a small bullet hole in the marble by the entrance to platform 1.

The Clock Tower

It wasn't until 1921 that the Clock Tower was built. Construction of the sandstone building, designed by eminent architects Philip Thalis and Peter John Cantrill started in 1901. It was designed to dominate the locality as a beacon, and remains one of the most identifiable landmarks.

A century before mobile phones and digital watches, commuters in Sydney depended on the Central Station clock tower for the accurate time. The clock tower was strategically placed to line up with many nearby streets including Broadway, Wentworth Avenue, Pitt, Valentine, Albion and Foveaux Streets. It has four faces, each of which is 4.77 metres in diameter, and the hour markings are 760 millimetres long. The 75 metre tall sandstone tower has stood grandly at the north-west corner of the station area visible to travellers and locals alike, and is certainly the most majestic of all the station clocks in Australia, and has been a Sydney landmark for the past century. Central Station is a significant terminal by world standards, equivalent to late Victorian and Edwardian stations in Europe. The 12th March 2021 marked the 100th birthday of this important Australian landmark (Australian Railway Historical Society, New South Wales Division, 2012).

The Mortuary Station

This railway building was intended for one unearthly purpose – to carry Sydney's deceased to their final resting place. Funeral trains, complete with hearse wagons laden with coffins left for Rookwood cemetery, not too far away.

Designed by the Colonial architect James Barnet, this splendid sandstone building still stands today, although it serves a different purpose. With its exquisitely worked arches and stonework, it remains a big part of Sydney's history to be enjoyed by the community. Hard sandstone was used for the columns, parapets and arches while the softer Pyrmont sandstone is used for the walls. The station has a slate roof while the octagonal entrance portico is dominated by a copper spire and outstanding carvings of leaves, angels and stars. In the 1980s, the station was heritage listed by the government, and restored to all its glory. Today, it commemorates not death but life (Sydney's Central, Australian Railway Historical Society, NSW Division, 2012).

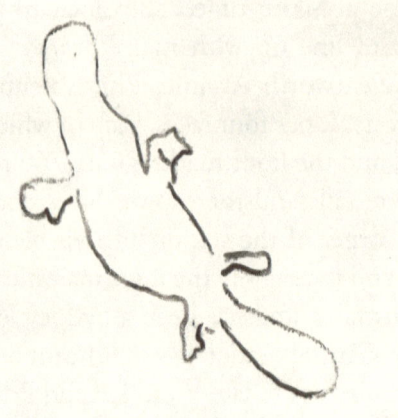

Note

Two-up. Two-up is a straightforward gambling game where coins (pennies) are tossed and bets are made on whether they will land on heads or tails. Pennies were used prior to decimalization in 1966. The "heads" refers to the coin used with the head of the Monarch – this could be King George VI or Queen Elizabeth II. The "tails" refers to the reverse of the coin, which is the Kangaroo.

The prize pool money is all the money invested by players. The spinner, (the person who tosses the coins) places two pennies on the kip (the kip means the wooden bat from which the pennies are thrown) and tosses them. The pennies must spin at least two metres over spinner's head and not come into contact with an object or a person. It must also land in the boundaries of the ring. Players bet on either two heads or two tails. The ringkeeper selects the spinner and controls the conduct of the game.

Under the Gambling (Two-up) Act 1998, the game can only be played on Anzac Day (April 25) all over Australia. In New South Wales and in some parts of other states, it can also be played on Victory in the Pacific Day (August 15) and Remembrance Day (November 11, but only after noon). You don't need a permit to play Two-up, but you need to be over 18 years of age. Of course, it can be played in private.

The origins of Two-up, date back to the trenches and troop ships during Gallipoli and the First World War; hence its association with Anzac Day.

CHAPTER 6

Melbourne

After Sydney, Melbourne is probably my favourite Australian city. Situated on the Yarra River, it is home to over 5,000,000 people. I love Melbourne's wide streets and lovely green gardens.

One cold, but sunny morning, I boarded the XPT at Sydney Central Station for my journey of 12 hours to Melbourne. The XPT is comfortable and travels at a leisurely speed through some of the most picturesque country you'll ever see. There are stops along the way, and they serve delicious scones with jam and cream for morning and afternoon teas. Hot lunches, sandwiches and snacks which can be taken to your seat, are available from the Buffet Car. The hours pass quickly as you chat with other passengers, or read a book or just sit and watch the countryside roll by.

We arrived at Melbourne's Southern Cross Station in the early evening. Long time friend Lia Cross came to meet me and I stayed at her place in Carlton North, for the duration of my holiday.

Despite the friendly rivalry between Sydney and Melbourne, the two cities have hosted the Olympics in 2000 and 1956 respectively. Nothing I had ever experienced prepared me for the awe inspiring view of Melbourne from the observation deck of the highest public vantage point in the Southern Hemisphere. Located on Level 88, Eureka Skydeck is Melbourne's 'must see' attraction. Skydeck 88 is the only observation deck in the world that can thrill you with the Edge – a glass cube which projects 3 metres out from the building, with you in it! Don't let the sound of the smashing and cracking glass make you nervous. I felt like fainting! It is perfectly placed on the banks of the Yarra River, and provides an incredible 360-degree view from the floor to the ceiling windows that overlook Melbourne's CBD, sports precinct, Port Phillip Bay, Docklands and everything inbetween. You feel that you're in seventh heaven as you absorb the jaw-dropping views that reach as far as the Dandenong Ranges by day, and at night see the beauty of the Melbourne Skyline.

Mention the Yarra River and you might think of the last few kilometres that cut through the city – but it's so much more. This iconic river flows 242 kilometres from its source on Mt. Baw Baw in the Yarra Ranges National Park, north-east of Melbourne, all the way to Port Phillip Bay. There's plenty of the Yarra to explore beyond the city. Melbourne's valuable natural asset is home to a range of beautiful Indigenous plants, animals, birds and fish, and is vital to the social and economic wellbeing. The Yarra River is the source of 70% of Melbourne's drinking water, supports productive agriculture and provides recreational opportunities like rowing, fishing, bird watching, picnicking and walking.

I wish more cities had a free tram service, but I was lucky to find this one in Melbourne. I'm not joking! It's the best deal in Melbourne – a hop on hop off tram service running through the city centre, taking you around the perimeter of the city and if you couple it with the regular tram, it's a great way to get around. It's an old-fashioned tram car, different from the numerous, modern, larger ones that run. There is a recorded, talking narration describing the areas you pass.

The well-known Queen Victoria Market is a genuine, buzzing, inner-city market that has been the essence of Melbourne for over 140 years. Home to over 600 small businesses, it's an amazing place to uncover fresh and speciality produce, hand-made and unique products, good Italian coffee and food, souvenirs and clothing. Shopping at the markets was one of life's delights for me, and it wasn't just the abundance of fresh food, it was the friendly repartee with the traders, the spirited and multicultural atmosphere, the special events and festivals and the sense of belonging that comes with it.

A visit to the Melbourne Cricket Ground, the MCG, the oldest and most popular sporting venue in Australia, is a must. It has hosted numerous international cricket matches, countless VFL/AFL Grand Finals, the 1956 Olympic Games and 2006 Commonwealth Games, at which I was present. Apart from its sporting events, the MCG has also witnessed many blockbuster music concerts, and Pope Paul 11 held a mass there when he visited Melbourne in 1986.

I would recommend a day at Sovereign Hill, it is a fantastic place to visit and we need to keep our Australian history alive. I had a wonderful time here, so much to see and do and Sovereign Hill brings to life the excitement of Australia's great 1850s gold rush named as Australia's best 'Major Tourist Attraction' four times. Federation Square boasts world-class galleries and facilities, a splendid and varied range of food, drink and sensational, extraordinary events – Fed Square is anything but square.

The Flinders Street railway station is located in the central business district. Opened in 1854, the historic station serves the entire metropolitan rail network, as well as some country services to eastern Victoria. Backing onto the Yarra River in the heart of the city, the complex includes platforms that stretch over more than two whole city blocks, from east of Swanton Street nearly to Market Street. It was the terminus of the first railway in Australia and was reputedly the world's busiest passenger station in the 1920s, owing to the concentration of the City Loop in the 1970s. Its main platform is Australia's longest, and the fourth longest railway platform in the world.

Melbourne is a blend of busy laneways, world-class restaurants, captivating museums and theatres. Her Majesty's Theatre is one of Melbourne's most iconic venues for live performances and has been entertaining Australia since 1886. To add that special something to your visit, Her Majesty's Theatre has elegantly appointed private rooms and catering options available for anywhere from couples celebrating a romantic night out at the theatre, through to large groups. The grand old dame of Melbourne theatres, the Princess dates back to 1886 but still hosts the hottest shows in town. With the gorgeous façade, domed roofs and marble foyer, this Victorian-era entertainment palace also boasts two dining rooms, the Melba and Marriner, for pre-show nibbles.

Opened in 2002, Birrarung Marr, was created as a place for the community and to celebrate public activities, major events and festivals. The park's name comes from the language of the Wurundjeri people who originally inhabited the area – 'birrarung' means 'river of mists' and 'Birrarung Marr translates to River Walk, or 'beside the river of mists' (Wikipedia, (2020, para. 6) states that….birrarung means "river of mists"). This park by the Yarra is a pleasant place to stroll. Many people don't realise that this is a sacred

Aboriginal site, is located on the Yarra River and is a traditional one because of the ceremonial importance that it conveys. Individuals from various tribes come to this location to perform a Tanderrum which is a large gathering. The images on the rocks are there to represent five different tribes of the creation spirit, Baiame and sky father in the Dreaming of several Aboriginal Australian peoples of south-eastern Australia, such as the Wonnarua, Kamilaroi, Eora, Darkinjung and Wiradjuri peoples.

Before European settlement, the Aboriginal people of the Wurundjeri Willum clan lived on the land that now forms the City of Whittlesea and the northern suburbs of Melbourne. They lived on the offshoots of the Yarra River – along the Merri, Edgars and Darebin Creeks, the Plenty River and the Maribyrnong River. The Wurundjeri clan spoke the Woi Wurrung language, and is one of the many language groups that make up the Kulin Nation, whose people shared the same religion and language, and lived in what is now metropolitan and greater Melbourne. The Wurundjeri people have always had a deep connection to the river. It provided the means and an important place for spiritual and community grounds. Many cultural sites are still there today – the Yarra Flats Dreaming, Bolin Bolin Billabong in Bulleen and the Heide Scar Tree. The Heide Scar Tree, known as Yingabeal, or songtree – Yinga means sing or song and beal is an Indigenous name for a redgum (Grace et al., 2016), represents an important link to Aboriginal cultural practices significant to the original inhabitants of the site, the Wurundjeri and Woiwurrung people, for whom this particular tree was a sacred ceremonial ground. Aboriginal people created scarred trees by removing bark from them to make containers, shields, canoes and to build temporary shelters. Before Heide became an art gallery, it was the home of John and Sunday Reed, who were patrons of the arts and arrived at the property in 1934 and created a place where artists could come to work. After they died, their house became the Heide Museum of Modern Art, a gallery that displays Australian art, including the collection that the Reeds built up in their lifetime. The Wurundjeri people have always had a deep connection to the river, which provided resources and important places for spiritual and community activity, like birthplaces and ceremonial and burial grounds. In 1835, Tasmanian farmer John Batman claimed he had bought the river and surrounding land from the Wurundjeri people in exchange for goods. However, the Wurundjeri believed that they had simply taken part in a friendship ceremony, and were granting Batman leave to pass through their country. The following year almost 200 Europeans had settled on the river's banks, growing to 500,000 people by 1860 once gold was discovered at one of the river's tributaries in Warrandyte. "Enthroned by gold', Melbourne quickly became Australia's largest city. But this expansion came at a cost. The former pristine Yarra soon became one of the world's dirtiest rivers – a place to dispose of all things unpleasant. Diseases like diphtheria, dysentery, typhoid and scarlet fever, were spread by the waters. Originally called Birrarung, meaning 'a place of mists and shadows'(Hyatt, Rob, (ND. para. 3) states that...." the Koorie Heritage Trust provides an opportunity for that voice....."). The river only became known as the Yarra in the 1830s, after a surveyor misheard local Aboriginal people saying Yarro Yarro: 'it flows'.

The Koorie Heritage Trust collections and walking tours captures Aboriginal history and is an important form of storytelling. As well as the Trust's incredible collection of art and artefacts, walking tours through Melbourne's significant Aboriginal sites are an important way to communicate culture with visitors. Rob Hyatt is the Cultural Education Manager for the Koorie Heritage Trust in Melbourne. He's

got a passion for Victoria's unique culture, and the importance of Aboriginal voice, identity, self-determination and
cultural expression. "The Heritage Trust provides an opportunity for that voice. We're here for all Aboriginal Victoria,
giving that voice of a continuous living culture", says Rob.

In early 1851, the Government announced that gold
had been discovered in Australia by Edward Hargreaves, John
Lister and William, James and Henry Tom, near Bathurst,
New South Wales. Gold was also discovered in Victoria in
June of that year. Gold was the stimulus for great change in
Australia. The belief that you could dig your own fortune
attracted people from across the country and around the
world. The call in London, California, Germany and Italy
was – 'off to the diggings'. On the 30th November 1854,
miners from the Victorian town of Ballarat, disgruntled with
the way the colonial Government had been administering
the goldfields, swore allegiance to the Southern Cross flag at
Bakery Hill and built a stockade at the nearby Eureka diggings. Early on the morning of Sunday 3rd December, when
the stockade was only lightly guarded, Government troops
attacked, and at least 22 diggers and six soldiers were killed.
Starting in 1853, the miners began to assemble at large meetings to voice their complaints, and delegations presented their
concerns to Governor La Trobe, but he was unresponsive to
their requests. The police were unsettled by the antagonism
among the diggers and decided to implement a licence hunt
the next day. That morning, as the police moved through
the miners' tents, the diggers decided they had had enough,
they gathered and marched on Bakery Hill, where the char-
ismatic Irishman Peter Lalor became the leader of the protest
and led the diggers to the area around Eureka. There, Lalor
supported by my namesake Raffaello Carboni (don't think
I'm related, but I've adopted him), led the men and women
in an oath: 'We swear by the Southern Cross, to stand truly

by each other, and fight to defend our rights and liberties' (Carboni, Raffaello, (1854, para. 6) states that...."we swear by the southern cross....").

Peter Lalor was born in Tinakill, Ireland, the son of a Home Rule supporter and landowner. He immigrated to Australia with one of his brothers in 1852, and found work on the Melbourne-Geelong railway and then at the Eureka gold-field in 1853. He joined the Ballarat Reform League, formed by miners in November 1854 to protest high licence fees, police ill-treatment, lack of representation and the scarcity of land. When the League's petition was ignored by the government, the miners organized to fight on November 30 and chose Lalor as their leader. Lalor and other rebels, including Raffaello Carboni, were driven out of the Eureka Stockade on December 3 and Lalor was wounded in the onslaught and lost an arm. Lalor went into hiding for several weeks and soon after when he emerged, the charges were dropped. After the miner's revolt, most of their complaints were redressed. He subsequently served in the Legislative Assembly in 1856-71 and 1875-87. In between his stretches of service int the legislature, Lalor worked as a land agent, was a director of minjing companies, served as Postmaster General (1875), Commissioner of Trade and Customs (1875, 1877-80), and speaker of the Assembly from 1880 to 1887, a position he resigned when his health worsened. He died on February 9, 1889.

Raffaello Carboni (1817 – 1875), linguist, traveller, author and composer, was born on 15th December 1817 at Urbino, Italy. In his teenage years, that impatience which characterised his later life was already evident. He attended the University of Urbino in 1835 – 36 but about 1837 moved to Rome where, with a recommendation from Prince Filippo Albani, he entered the seminary of Santa Trinità. Suspected of collaborating with the French republicans, he was imprisoned briefly in 1840 but, according to his own account, was immediately released when the papal authorities realised that petty spite rather than genuine suspicion had prompted a superior to report him. At this time he developed his talent for learning languages. Carboni learnt French, German, Spanish and took English lessons from W. Vincent Eyre, vice-rector of the English College in Rome. He lived mainly in London, until, in 1852 was attracted, like many others, by articles, particularly those in the Illustrated London News, on the gold discoveries in Australia and set sail for Melbourne. Carboni began his career as a digger at Ballarat and had immediate success at Golden Point, but early in 1853 he moved with many others to Magpie Gully. However, when his washing was stolen, his comrades and he decided to part company; the flies got in his eyes an after a bad bout of dysentery he made up his mind to turn shepherd. He was less successful at sheep tender than he was a digger, and after briefly living with an Aboriginal tribe he succumbed again to gold fever and returned to Ballarat. Until then, he had paid little attention to the deafening complaints about the price of licences. He had attended meetings, in particular one at Bakery Hill in November 1853. In this second period as a digger he was caught up in events and stayed to contribute no mean part to the Eureka revolt. He was described as shrewd and restless with reddish hair and red beard cut short, and small hazel eyes that had a fiery twinkle beneath a broad forehead and rather shaggy eyebrows. An articulate European, he was a controversial figure among the miners. He was appointed by Peter Lalor, whom he admired, to organise the foreigners behind the stockade and was in a small group who went to the camp to petition for the discontinuance of licence hunting. As a member in the inner committee, he was charged with high treason but acquitted since no jury would convict them.

That morning almost 300 mounted and foot troopers, and police attacked the stockade. The assault was over in 15 minutes, with at least 22 diggers (including one woman) and six soldiers lost their lives. The police arrested and detained 113 of the miners, 13 of whom were taken to Melbourne to stand trial. Governor Hotham called for a Goldfields Commission of Enquiry on 7th December, but the citizens of Victoria were opposed to what the Government had done in Ballarat and one by one the 13 leaders of the rebellion were tried by jury and released. In March the Commission of Enquiry released their recommendations. The licence fee was removed, replaced by an export duty and a nominal £1 per year miners' right. Half the police on the goldfields were sacked and one warden replaced the multitude of gold commissioners who had issued the licences, many of whom were corrupt. Twelve new members were added to the Victorian Legislative Council, four appointed by the Queen and eight elected by those diggers who held a miner's right. One of these members was Peter Lalor who had survived the Eureka clash but had been wounded in the left arm, which was later amputated.

Lalor's supporter Raffaello Carboni, was elected with nine others on 14th July 1855 to the new local court at Ballarat, he made forceful contributions on the question of legal representation in the court. He delayed his departure from Australia in order to write the account of the stockade as a tribute to those who fell and as a vindication of his own name. The book, now rare was sold by 'fiery lachrymose, faithful Raffaello' on the first anniversary of the stockade.

It was a victory for the miners and was one of the key steps to Victoria instituting male suffrage in 1857 and female suffrage in 1908.

CHAPTER 7

The Ghan Expedition

The Ghan is an odd name for a train, in Australian history it is a living legend for it's the ultimate journey through the heart of the continent. The legendary Ghan takes you from the coast of Adelaide to the coast of Darwin, or visa versa, over three awe-inspiring days and two relaxing nights, into the heart of Australia. One hundred and fifty years ago, the first camels were imported along with their handlers from Afghanistan and, in true Australian style, the name was soon shortened to the 'Ghan'. The camels of today are descended from these camels and carry supplies through the interior of the continent. Originally named the Afghan Express, the Ghan was named to pay tribute to the Afghan Camel Drivers who provided invaluable help navigating and exploring Australia's centre in the early 1900s. Over the years, this explanation has often been disputed, with suggestions that the name was invented by railwaymen on the line as a private staff joke to the detriment of Commonwealth Railways Commissioner George Gahan, who was responsible for creating and running the iconic railway service.

Commissioner Gahan was not popular with the staff. They referred to the Ghan as the Gahan Express behind his back, placing stress on the word "express" as the train was notorious for being slow, and was often anywhere up to a few days late. Whether the train was named after the Afghan camel drivers or the unloved Commissioner Gahan, remains the subject for discussion. The Ghan's symbol is an Afghan pioneer on a camel in recognition of the 19th century Afghan cameleers' efforts in opening up the harsh interior to the rest of Australia; but for these camels, well-fed tourists are the only burden they carry today. Large numbers of feral camels roam free throughout inland Australia. Today one can make this journey with creature comforts that the ancestors would never have imagined.

Boarding The Ghan in Adelaide for Alice Springs and Darwin, one experiences one of the most fascinating great train journeys of the world. There is also a 4 day/3 night Ghan expedition tour which includes an enhanced off train excursion in Katherine, extra time in Alice Springs, and an off train excursion in Coober Pedy. Of the 35,000 to 40,000 people who ride The Ghan every year, about 80 per cent are Australian, and although the demographic skews older, it's great fun whatever your age. In my carriage there was a woman travelling solo for her 39th birthday, another celebrating her 80th, a couple of sisters on a trip in memory of their mum, and a retired banker of 65 years old. This 2979 km journey guides you deep into the heart of Australia, making stops at Manguri (Coober Pedy), Alice Springs, Tenant Creek, Katherine and Darwin.

The first time I travelled on The Ghan it went from Sydney to Alice Springs. The line from Alice Springs was opened in 2004, and I was lucky enough to be on it in the first service. The train had been booked out for over two years, everybody wanted to get on it and as we travelled along, there were lots of people on the overhead bridges taking photos of the train which was over a kilometre long, with two locomotives. It's not long after boarding the Ghan that I began to appreciate why the romance of train travel endures.

Rumbling out of Adelaide on a wintery morning, it's hard not to be overcome by the excitement of a journey that's on the "bucket list" of so many travellers. We were treated like kings with the usual delicious food and wine and plenty of freebees - dressing gown, slippers, toiletries bag and a map of the route. The staff were an absolute delight, so helpful, and always with a smile. The Ghan is known for luxury, but it wasn't always so. The original trains were far more practical, used largely for freight and transport. Flying may be quicker, and more convenient, but there's something about trains that allows the traveller to embrace the maxim: life's a journey, not a destination. Once I had settled into my private cabin, I mingled with fellow travellers in the lounge before a regionally-inspired lunch accompanied by a selection of all-inclusive wines and beverages. Yes, again. I didn't know if I could have kept up with all this pampering! The trip was unparalleled and not the usual journey where you sit or sleep in your carriage waiting to get to your destination. You spend time mingling with some great people.

The red centre of Australia is an iconic destination and one that draws scores of tourists to Australian shores each year. The heart of Australia and one of the most renowned natural landmarks in Australia is a sight to behold. Travelling through the centre of Australia can be done in a number of ways but a truly unique experience is taking The Ghan from Adelaide to Darwin which is sure to leave lasting memories for the most seasoned traveller. Travelling almost 3000 kilometres, The Ghan is a monumental trip that takes on average 54 hours to complete. Each stop along the way offers an opportunity for a traveller to break up the journey with an overnight stay to experience more of the stunning desert landscapes found in each stop.

Ron Dadleh, a descendent of the Afghan cameleers helped build the train line to Alice Springs. Ron and his wife Sue dreamt of travelling on The Ghan for its 90th birthday but sadly, he passed away a month before their 51st wedding anniversary. Graham Dadleh, Ron's nephew drove the train from Port Augusta to Pimba for its 90th anniversary on the 4th August 2019. Trains have been in the Dadleh family since the cameleers began building the tracks. Ron was an inspector on the railways and the last station manager, in an acting capacity, at Marree which closed in 1980 when a new standard gauge line bypassed the town.

Our next stop was Manguri for the Coober Pedy excursion, the name is a combination of two Aboriginal words, Kupaka and Piti, which, combined mean a white man in a hole. Approximately 150 million years ago, (I am at a loss as to how this is calculated) the ocean covered the Coober Pedy region. As the sea water receded, climatic changes caused the lowering of the underground water tables. Silica solutions were carried down to deposit in cavities, faults and fractures in the ground and now, millions of years later, these silica solutions have formed into opal. For thousands of years, Aboriginal people, who were nomadic hunters, walked across this area, constantly in search of food and well to attend traditional ceremonies. In 1975 the Coober Pedy Aboriginal Community adopted the name "Umoona", meaning "long life" (Coober Pedy History, (September, 2021, para. 2) states that…Umoona means "long life…"). The name is also used for the "Umoona" or mulga tree; a common tree in this area. Coober was originally known as the Stuart Range Opal Field, named after John McDouall Stuart who, in 1858, was the first European explorer to visit the area. In 1920 a new name was chosen. The discovery of opal in 1945 by Toddy Bryant, an Aboriginal woman, caused widespread public excitement and changed the course of events, which went a long way towards cementing the future prosperity of Coober Pedy. Coober Pedy was discovered early in 1915 by a 14-year-old boy. It is the world's largest opal bearing region and produces 80% of Australia's opal.

In 1956, a gem named "Olympus Australis" by Frank Tethridge and Bert Wilson who discovered this 143 ounce opal was sold to Greg Sherman, the son of John and Georgina Sherman who migrated to Australia in 1891 from England and started the "dynasty" of an opal family that survives to the third generation. Third generation Sherman Peter Sherman was born in Sydney and began his interest in opals at the age of 10, and continues today. Frank Tethridge tells of how they discovered the famous opal – "Bert Wilson was an experienced miner from Amdamooka and Coober Pedy who had been involved in Aboriginal lady Toddy Bryant's Eight Mile rush. An elderly man lived in a dugout next to me and was known locally as the King of Opal and could almost smell opal in the ground. At that time, I knew little about the game, as I had been on the field only a few months when we teamed up to work together. He took me out to the Eight Mile where two of his teenage sons had been working some 20-foot ground seven years earlier but had pulled out after they discovered a large brown snake in the mine".

While Coober Pedy's main attraction is opal, the town is sometimes seen as a stopover destination. But things are changing, says local lady Deb. "We're seeing the overnight stays getting longer and all these advantages that we're creating in the town are giving people a reason to stay longer". Deb says that business confidence in Coober Pedy is high and the history tours, noodling areas, underground churches, underground mine museum and the Dingo Fence – the world's longest fence" are attracting tourists as well as interest in opals. In the four years to 2016, about 103,000 international and domestic overnight visitors came to Coober Pedy, and together poured $31 million into the local economy.

Along the way we sighted kangaroos, emus, wallabies and yes, camels. We alighted the train at Marla in South Australia, which marks the start of the remote Oodnadatta Track, to watch the sunrise and enjoy a light breakfast in the heart of the outback. At Marla, I joined a tour to the three tracks, the Oodnadatta, Birdsville and Strzelecki.

Oodnadatta is a small remote town and locality in South Australia about 873 kilometres north of Adelaide, which lies in the heart of the desert 112 metres above sea level. It is , by any description a captivating place which, since the closure of the railway line in 1981, has become a quiet settlement inhabited by Aborigines who run the Ra Museum, the General Store and the local Transcontinential Hotel built in the 1890s, located near the famous Pink Road House along with the caravan park.

The Pink Roadhouse

The Pink Roadhouse, a popular tourist attraction (so named because it is painted bright pink), is a place to stop, and the museum in the old railway station offers an understanding about the hardships tolerated by Europeans who ventured into this inhospitable land. It provides petrol, a general store, meals, a variety of accommodation and post office facilities. The Pink Roadhouse was established by Adam Plate and Lynnie Trevellian in 1983. In the summer of 1974, Greg McHugh walked into Oodnadatta with two aboriginal blokes called Nugget and Jimmie from Hermannsburg, west of Alice Springs, and some camels, horses and donkeys, on their way to Gulgong, a few thousand kilometres to the east. With his was his girlfriend Cassi Pate, her brother Adam and Adam's girlfriend Lynnie Trevellian. Greg was returning home, the aborigines were heading out on an adventure, and Sydney types with them and Canberra type Lynnie, though not a public servant, were on a sort of backpacker meandering, looking for the meaning of life, as one did in the 70s. After an altercation with Greg, Adam returned to the shining streets of the village vowing to put his own team together. There were thousands of donkeys around the mainly unfenced local cattle stations. Oodnadatta was a railway town in those days, aborigines were allowed to drink and vote, and the town had an interesting sparkle after dusk as port and Southwark Bitter bottles banging created a symphonic music to accompany the rowdy street theatre of public altercation and dangerous assault. In 1978, Adam started a motorbike repair business and his experience with riding BMW bikes, came in handy. Later Lynnie and Adam started a part time snack bar called the Tuckerbox which became the first soup kitchen feeding hungry kids who would uselessly wait for parents to leave the pub with enough money for dinner. Lynnie's start into retailing was because a traveller couldn't buy a cup of tea easily at that time in Oodnadatta. Then non-drunk travellers started to appear, in contrast to the stockmen in town on a booze-up for the rail fettler from one of the many nearby maintenance gangs. The Tuckerbox had Oodnadatta's first jukebox and only opened when the main town store, owned by the well known Czech entrepreneur, the late Jaroslav Pecanec, closed. When Lynnie's father gave her a 1969 Dodge Phoenix vehicle, Adam had it spray painted bright pink and parked it in front of the store. Subsequently, he painted everything pink, and called it the Pink Roadhouse. Lynnie said, 'the Pink Roadhouse is here to make you smile and make you feel at ease, to help you enjoy your stay in the outback', (Lynnie Trevellian, (2005, para. 15) states that…."the Pink Roadhouse is here…"). The Pink Roadhouse has post office facilities and most importantly a toll-free phone for travellers trying to deal with the miss-information and lack of interest in the outback shown by the city-state governors down south.

The opportunity of taking over ownership of this icon proved too much for Ian and Cathie King, and Jennifer and Peter Moore. Continuing the legacy of Adam (who died on the 30th August, 2012), and Lynnie Plate, the new owners want to help people enjoy the outback. "Our vision and passion is to help people enjoy this remarkable outback area and to maintain the legacy of Adam and Lynnie Plate and the Pink Roadhouse", Mrs. King said. "Ian and I have been wandering around the remote areas of Australia for the past 30 years", she goes on to say. "We were married in Victoria in 1984, when Ian was working in the High Country as a forester for the Victorian Forests Commission and I was managing the office at the Mount Buffalo Chalet. We moved to the Northern Territory and brought up our two children. Our interests strayed from this type of work when we owned and managed the Family Hotel at Tibooburra in New South Wales. At the same time, Peter Moore ran the William Creek Hotel, where we were able to feed travellers with discouraging comments about each other!". When our children left the nest and we were seeking some adventure, the opportunity arose to move to Oodnadatta with Jen and Peter and get involved with the Pink Roadhouse. We believe it is an absolute icon of the outback and we jumped at the chance. We are excited to live and be part of the community of Oodnadatta. With the fabulous history of Oodnadatta and the adventure of the Australian Outback beckoning Adam's phrase will be our motto: Pink Roadhouse – your mates in the bush".

Oodnadatta has a hot desert climate and has recorded the highest reliably measured maximum temperature in Australia of 50.7C on the 2nd January 1960.

The Transcontinental Hotel, imagine, an international sounding name in the middle of nowhere! A truly Australian pub, and the meals were great. We were warmly welcomed to this especially pleasant place with fabulous country service and an extensive pub menu with a surprisingly fine wine list with just enough variety to make it interesting (can't go past Taylors Cab Sav or Shiraz). Every aspect of this marvellous pub was a delight. This one for the bucket list.

Some 400 camels were stationed here during the 1890's tended by Muslim cameleers, known in Australia as Afghans, who played an intrinsic role in pioneering the Red Centre. The name, Oodnadatta, (sounds remote doesn't it?), probably originates from the Arrernte word utnadata, meaning mulga blossom. It was for tens of thousands of years a stop on an old trade route for Aboriginal people. It is likely that the unsealed Oodnadatta Track, 620 kilometres of legendary outback track from Marree to Marla, predates the arrival of Europeans by tens of thousands of years. The track closely follows the paths taken by explorers Stuart and Giles searching inland Australia during the 1800s. It was a trade route for the local Aborigines who moved from spring to spring along a route which was eventually to be used for both the Overland Telegraph Line and the railway to Alice Springs. Railway relics, mostly sleepers, lie alongside the track between Marree and William Creek. The rich colour and roughness of the terrain, personified by the remoteness of the Australian Outback, encourages the enthusiastic adventurer to discover the real charm of this region. There's more to it than just a great outback track. For a start there's artesian hot springs to swim in and great waterholes to camp at and some incredibly picturesque places. Then there is the track's history to explore. You're following the route of the original old Ghan Railway from Adelaide to Alice Springs, so there are plenty of historic railway sidings and buildings to stop and inspect. Along the way, the Track passed Lake Eyre, and we stopped for a quick drink and a bite to eat in William Creek, all the time following the historic route of the old Ghan railway. The Track also passes by the largest cattle station in the world: Anna Creek and some of the world's most unique desert features: mound springs. Mound springs take their name from the peculiar mounds that build up around some springs. With water flowing from the top of the mound and out onto the surrounding plains, they form a truly bizzare landscape. The springs can be fresh or salty, and can be warm or even hot, as the water comes from deep underground where it is heated by the earth's cover and high pressures. The cooler part of the year is the perfect time to visit mound springs in South Australia's desert parks. They are true oases in the desert, providing a lifeline for people and animals alike. The Dalhousie Springs, in South Australia's far north-east, is made up of 148separate springs, all nourished by the Great Artesian Basin, an enormous underground water source that flows under nearly a fifth of the country. The springs have been flowing here for between one and two million years and are home to a huge diversity of fauna found nowhere else on the planet. Of cultural significance to local Aboriginal people, these springs have been the only reliable permanent water sources in the arid outback since humans first arrived in the region.

Anna Creek Station, which covers 15,746 square kilometres, is situated 160 kilometres east of Coober Pedy and midway between Oodnadatta and Marree. The station was relocated to its present site in approximately 1872 (from Stangways Springs), and in 1935, after several different owners, Anna Creek became part of the Kidman Holdings, joining the already owned Stuarts Creek Station and The Peake Station. Anna Creek became the headquarters of the giant pastoral block under the management of the McLean and the Nunn families, an association that continued for 100 years. In December 2016, the Williams Cattle Company acquired Anna Creek Station along with The Peake Station.

We arrived at William Creek, the smallest settlement in South Australia with a population of 3 humans and a dog! We stayed overnight at the William Creek Pub Hotel, the middle of nowhere in the outback. The room wasn't luxurious by any stretch of the imagination, but it was comfortable and clean, and did its job. The staff were very friendly and welcoming and the meals were wonderful and it was a great atmosphere. It was a delight to spend the short time there. I joined a flight over Lake Eyre which is the best thing to do to see the magnificent lake with its incredible colours and patterns. We continued exploring the Oodnadatta Track that morning and then headed south towards Marree.

We checked in at the Marree Pub Hotel for our overnight accommodation. No outback adventure is complete without a stay at the Marree Pub Hotel. More than just a hotel, built in 1883, this Award Winning Hotel is where your outback odyssey begins. You do need a lot of time however, and we did not on this occasion – a future travel destination. The walls of the hotel are adorned with photos of Donald Campbell's 1964 world record run on Lake Eyre. Phil, Maz and Joe made sure our visit was beyond our expectations – great rooms, great bar staff, quintessential hospitality, the stories, superb food, museums full of local history, characters and, when you leave, you will have experienced something unique – classic outback accommodation, the coldest beer anywhere and unparalleled hospitality. Copy that! I would not hesitate to return and stay again.

The Indigenous people of the Lake Ayre region are the Arabunna. Reg Dodd is a genuinely fascinating Aboriginal Elder, and his tours include opportunities to explore and learn about local Aboriginal culture, tradition, sacred sites and rock arts as well as trips to the edge of Lake Eyre. While travelling along the fabled Oodnadatta Track you encounter the ancient, natural wonders of the Lake Eyre Basin while sampling bush tucker and discovering bush medicines and other desert resources. The mysterious image of a giant Aboriginal man scraped into the desert puts Marree on the map in 1998. Now the enormous second-largest geoglyph has made a return, locals hope he'll once again prove to be a drawcard. Unlike the 1000-year old Nazca Lines in Peru that hold the title of the biggest geoglyphs, the artwork has become known as the Marree Man is more of recent beginning. Located 60 kilometres north-west of Marree, the 4.2 kilometre long work, was first sighted from the air by a local pilot in 1998. Local pub-owner Phil Turner bought the Marree Pub Hotel seven years ago partly on the potency of the Marree Man. "I got carried away, like everyone else, with the myth, the mystery and the intrigue, the fact they couldn't find the people who did it", he says. "The Marree Man was such an attraction – scenic flights were helping business – and it was part of our decision to buy the pub". Theories about who made it bounded and grew in all different directions. Inquiries focused briefly around the US Army, thanks to the Man's closeness to the joint US-Australian defence projects of the Woomera Prohibited Area. The investigation was closed in April with the change of government, and Phil can relax at last. "It cost me $50,000 in legal fees. Am I a happy chappy about that? No, I'm not, but if you ask me if I'd do it again – yes, I would. It was the right thing to do". Having done it, he's guaranteed that the Marree Man can reach maturity in peace, a sleeping giant bringing life to the desert.

I was staggered by the changing colours as the sun set over Wilpena Pound and the Flinders Ranges. Rugged, ancient and harsh, is how I would describe the Oodnadatta Track. However, for me, it had been one of the highlights of that trip.

We reboarded the train in the late afternoon and travelled north through the desert while enjoying dinner in the train's Queen Adelaide Restaurant.

Alice Springs is an obvious tourist stop to see while travelling on the Ghan. When you descend from The Ghan at Alice Springs railway station, everything assumes a different dimension. You realise that those hills that looked so quaint when viewed through the picture windows of The Ghan are actually quite high and rugged. Alice Springs is located in the middle of the Mcdonnell Ranges. Once truly Himalayan in proportions, millions of years of erosion have reduced them to little more than skeltons of their former grandness. Aside from Uluru, Alice Springs, known by the locals as The Alice, has some sights that are much closer than The Rock. Surrounded by yellow sands and enchantingly beautiful mountain ranges, Alice Springs is a city with perhaps surprising events, arts and culture despite its remoteness.

The Todd River flows almost through the centre of the town. It is a transient river being in an arid part of Australia and has no water or very little during 95% of the year. They say that if you see the Todd River flow through Alice Springs three times, you'll never leave. For most of the year, its river-bed is as dry as a bone, and if you want to see the river flow in earnest on three separate occasions, you'll need to mark time for an eon! The Indigenous Arrernte people know this river as Lhere Mparntwe, here we go; pronounced ler-ra m-barn-twa. The Todd River's English name, and that of its tribu-tary, the Charles River, were given by surveyor W.W.Mills, after Charles Todd, then South Australian Superintendent of Telegraphs and Postmaster General of South Australia, who was largely responsible for the construction of the overland telegraph line.

The Australian Overland Telegraph Line was 3,200 kilo-metres that connected Darwin with Port Augusta in South Australia. Completed 1872, the Overland Telegraph Line allowed permitted fast communication between Australia and the rest of the world. The contract stated the line would be built by 1st January 1872 with a budget of £128,000. South Australia hoped that by being the first point of contact between Australia and the rest of the world would stimulate the colony's business environment.

The Henley on Todd Regatta is the world's only dry river bed boating regatta. It takes place every year on the third Saturday in August and it's the day of fun, hilarity and plenty of laughs. Nothing stops the sports, and the beer-loving peo-ple of Alice Springs a good time. The 'boats' are bottom-less and the crews race barefoot with their lightweight craft hauled up around their waists. No oars, coxes or winged keels are required here, just a swift pair of heels. The boats come in all shapes and sizes – yachts with sails, kayaks, flat-bottom boats pushed through the sand using shovels instead of oars, and even a bathtub derby where contestants carry a passenger in a tub. There's plenty of lawlessness away from the bathtub action. Locals put on peculiar outfits, a procession of boats and floats winds its way through the streets and, in proper outback style, enough booze to fill the Todd. One of the most famous fixtures in a country obsessed by sport, the event began, like many great Australian traditions, as a mockery. In this case, the target was the regatta on Henley-on-Thames, where the English upper class scoffs champagne and strawberries. If you are a spectator, then you'll have a marvelous day watching all kinds of crazy races in the regatta – just make sure you drink plenty of water and have lots of sun protection, the Alice Springs climate is harsh and relentless, and if you go unprepared you won't be spared! If you are a participant, then heavens help you. It's a dangerous event – ships can collapse and topple and any manner of mishaps can descend on you.

Myrtle Noske grew up next to the Todd River. She was born at Deep Well Station in 1926. Her father, the early pioneer Geerhardt Johannsen built the family home on what is now the Todd Mall. He moved the family to town when the cattle station ran out of water. Myrtle was eighteen months old when she arrived in Alice Spring . The house was opposite Adelaide House on a large block adjacent to the river, perfectly located for easy access to the river. "As soon as the Todd was starting to run we'd be all down there paddling in the muddy water. Of course we'd come home covered in hives and with skin irritation from all of the caterpillar dust that's in the water" (Noske, (1930, para. 4) states that…"as soon as the river started to run…"), said Myrtle. Myrtle died on 20th February, 2020 aged 94.

Breathtaking national parks and gardens such as the MacDonnell Ranges, where you can take a helicopter ride, the Alice Springs Desert Park and the Olive Pink Botanic Gardens are a must to visit when in Alice Springs. These locations provide a fantastic glimpse at the natural environment of this harsh landscape. A morning or afternoon here gives you a brief view into the history of yesterday and the unique lifestyle of today. At the Desert Park view a spectacular bird show, and listen to stories of the desert that helps you to appreciate and enjoy this beautiful landscape. On a characteristic day at the park you can expect to learn how Aboriginal people found food or medicines in the desert, and how to identify some of the important plants and animals they use. You can catch a glimpse of the Centre's history back through four and a half billion years (give or take a million or two) – there we go again, how on earth is this calculated!

Over 10 days each September, singers, musicians and audiences from Alice Springs and Central Australia and visitors to the region experience an exceptional festival. The Desert Song Festival is a tradition with a vision – choirs from the spirited multi-cultural community come together to present a series of events that showcase the singer and the song. The Asante Sana and other Alice Springs – based choirs, smaller ensembles, individual performers and groups from different sacred music traditions come together in a number of events in a celebration of the singer and the song through major concerts, chamber concerts, workshops, a Festival Club and an 'open stage'. Aboriginal traditional and sacred music, African freedom songs, ballads, classical compositions, Caribbean folk music, and a capella singing make their appearance on the cultural buffet that is Central Australia. The 'Centrepiece' of the Festival is a musical work: "Desert Dreaming", a rather autobiographical choral fantasia sourced by life and experiences in Central Australia 1995-2015, featuring Desert Choirs, musicians, dancers and rear projection.

The Olive Pink Opera, produced by the Olive Pink Botanic Garden, is a showcase event of the Desert Song Festival. Performed under the stars in the garden, the enchantment of this ground-breaking event is a first for Alice Springs and a first for the Desert Song Festival. The Opera celebrates the powerful and extraordinary life of Olive Pink, a remarkable woman, whose relationships with Arrernte and Warlpiri peoples and her outspoken advocacy for Aboriginal rights in Central Australia, is based on stories from both Aboriginal and local non-Aboriginal people from Alice Springs. It is a reconciliation work that tells of these stories, which strengthens communities in Alice Springs and indeed, the Australian community. The ground-breaking event of the Olive Pink Opera is a first for Alice Springs and a first for the Desert Song Festival.

The Alice Springs Reptile Centre contains the largest collection of reptiles in the Northern Territory. Animals at the centre include, frill-necked lizards, thorney devils, large and small pythons, brown snakes, death adders and king brown snakes. Be sure to visit this popular tourist destination, which devoted to Indigenous reptiles. Many are collected from local properties or from areas about to be burned under the controlled burning program to keep bushfires from threatening local homes. The Alice Springs Reptile Centre also doubles as a snake call centre, with the owner and staff going out to homes to remove venomous snakes from places where they might trouble people. Eek!

Pyndan Camel Tracks is another must see and do activity when travelling through the Northern Territory. They are the only camel riding tour operators in Alice Springs, situated in the beautiful White Gums Valley, among the MacDonnell Ranges. Their featured sunset tour against the backdrop of the incredible West MacDonnell Ranges is very much recommended.

I went to Alice Springs for one, a slightly odd reason: the Alice Springs Camel Cup which is an annual camel racing festival held at Blatherskite Park five kilometres from the Alice Springs CBD, on a winter Saturday. The first such event was held in 1970 in the dry bed of the Todd River and soon became a part of the Alice Springs Centenary Year Celebrations. The Camel Cup is one of the most bizarre events on the outback calendar, and here I met characters as authentically Australian as they come. Around 20 camels and their riders travel from farms around the region and race eight heats, leading up to a finale. But the event is more than a competition, It's a carnival and an unconventional one at that. Often hailed as the Melbourne Cup of camel racing, the Alice Springs Camel Cup draws thousands of tourists and spectators annually, each keen to catch a glimpse of the action and a mouthful of red dust. Behind the gangling animals are the cameleers of Central Australia who bring it all to life. The Stuarts Well Camel Farm, owned by Neil and Jayne Waters, about 90 kilometres from Alice Springs, has supplied camels for the famous outback race. "It's just good fun, a good day out for the camels to stretch their legs and make a little bit of money for some local charities" (Burke, (2019, para. 9) states that…."It's just good fun, a good day out…"). Mr. Waters said. All joking aside, the couple have claimed so many trophies over the years for training and riding champion camels, that they no longer fit in their trophy cabinets!

About 3 hours and 27 minutes drive from Alice Springs is Kings Canyon where, if you make the effort and make the steep climb to the rim, you have a spectacular view of Watarrka National Park. For an exceptional experience wake before dawn and rise quietly into the fresh morning air in a hot air balloon. Experience one of the most popular Australian outback escapades where you'll get a bird's eye view of the majestic landscapes and wildlife. Drift silently alongside the rugged West MacDonnell Ranges and watch the sunrise spread out across desert oaks and mulga scrub. Keep an eye out for native wildlife, including wallabies and mighty red kangaroos.

With its remote outback location, it's not surprising that Alice Springs dazzles and delights when it comes to sky-watching. We observed the magic of the Milky Way with a glass of champagne on an astronomical encounter at the Earth Sanctuary. The night started with drinks and the local craft beer and the quandong (bush peach) available at the bar. As the night rolled on, a selection of the local bush tucker canapès was served while viewing the infinite desert expanse. As darkness emerges and the sun finally sets over the majestic MacDonnell Ranges, the star gazing experience went cosmic. The knowledgeable star guide explained the magic of the zodiacs and constellations with a laser-guided journey through the southern night sky. After dessert, we were introduced to the Earth Sanctuary Observatory and telescope viewing of celestial highlights on this occasion.

The Todd Mall comes alive with the Todd Mall Markets, an essential part of Alice Springs and the community – shops and markets will be the death of me! It has been a popular venue for tourists and locals for over 20 years. I found all kinds of treasures and was able to chat with the stallholders and locals. One of the friendlier groups you'll ever find.

Alice Springs is known as a small town with big heart and the gateway to the Northern Territory's ancient outback. The Alice epitomizes the consummate Australian spirit that is intertwined into the stuff-of-life here. My Alice encounter left me with an impression of the very best kind.

Simpson's Gap is one of the most prominent gaps in the West MacDonnell Ranges and is located 18 kilometres by a sealed road from Alice Springs, it features the towering cliffs of Simpsons Range, a permanent waterhole, and opportunities to spot resident wildlife. An illusory location where important factors of flora, fauna and Indigenous culture all come together, the Simpsons Gap area constitutes large stands of Mulga and is a major stronghold for over 40 rare and relict plants. You can enjoy walks that pass the native plants of the area including ancient Ghost Gums and views of the range.

Known as Rungutjirpa to the Arrernte Aboriginal people, Simpsons Gap was the mythological home of a group of giant goanna ancestors. Several dreaming tales and stories cross at this important spiritual site. The serenity and peaceful feeling as you watch the walls glow from reflected sunlight, creating a breath-taking display of stark form and rich colour, will leave you spellbound. I certainly was rendered motionless.

We raced through Tennant Creek the next morning during breakfast. The discovery of gold saw the establishment of the township. Aboriginal people have lived in this region for over 40,000 years and this area was used by the Warumingu people during times of drought due to the presence of permanent water holes. When the Tennant Creek Telegraph station was built in the 1870's, the Warumungu people experienced their first interactions with Europeans, some worked for the station and received rations. On another occasion I returned to Tennant Creek where I stopped by the Nyinkka Nyunyu Art and Culture Centre, displaying the ways of the Warumungu people, whose legend states that Tennant Creek is within the homeland of the powerful ancestral being, Nyinkka, a spiky tailed goanna. Fascinating!

North of Tennant Creek is the Pink Palace, originally built as a hostel for stockmen and their families, but today it ishome to the Julalikari Arts and Crafts program, where local Aboriginal women meet to paint traditional and contemporary artwork.

Not far from there are the famous Devils Marbles in the Devils Marbles Conservation Reserve – and what a spectacular sight to behold. It takes 58 minutes to drive from Tennant Creek to the Devils Marbles. Of course you can join a tour group, as I did, and travel by coach. There are several companies that conduct tours. According to Warumungu mythology, the "Marbles" are the eggs of the Rainbow Serpent. The smaller relatives of the Devils Marbles, The Pebbles form a unique and beautiful landscape. These granite boulders are know to the Warumungu Aboriginal people as Kunjarra, and are a sacred site and women's dancing place for the Munga Munga Dreaming where ritual instruction of young girls takes place.

The area around Tennant Creek was home to cattle king, Peter Sherwin who died at age 88, built a cattle empire which at one time was greater than Kidman and Co (Kidman and Co Pty Ltd is one of Australia's largest beef producers with a herd of 171,000 cattle). At the height of their pastoral career, Peter and Florrie Sherwin's landholding grew in the late 1970's and the 1980's. They managed and transported unforeseen stock numbers and was responsible for the massive and innovative infrastructure upgrades and developments which are still in use across northern cattle stations today.

The Ghan these days frequently passes Marla (159 kilometres south of the Northern Territory border), which is primarily a service town to the Ghan. Situated east of the Anangu Pitjantjatjara lands in South Australia, the Traveller's Rest is very much the heart of Marla. This sprawling roadhouse, hotel/motel, restaurant, service station, supermarket and much more provides travellers and locals with a comprehensive range of facilities. There are also camping grounds a caravan park and a health centre operated by the Royal Flying Doctor Service of Australia on behalf of the Northern Territory Government. There is also an airport – known as the Marla Aerodrome. The official population is just over 100 people.

And now to Katherine, population of 6,303 people according to the 2016 census. Katherine lies alongside the Katherine River at the junction of the Victoria Highway and the Stuart Highway, approximately 270 kilometres southeast of Darwin. The first inhabitants of the area were Indigenous Australian tribes, specifically the Dagoman people, Jawoyn people and Wardaman people. Kakadu has been home to Aboriginal people for more than 65,000 years and the culture is strong. The Aboriginal ancestors were hunter-gatherers, and as the seasons changed, they moved around the park to find food and comfort.

We arrived early the next morning and began our excursion to Nitmiluk National Park and the cruise on the Katherine River in the Katherine Gorge. The Katherine River was explored in 1862 by John McDouall Stuart, who named it after the daughter of one of his patrons. The town began as a repeater station for the Overland Telegraph Line, which reached the site in 1871. During World War 11, Katherine was a military base. The Australian Army set up two hospitals around Katherine, the 101st Australian General Hospital and 121st Australian General Hospital. The army also set up a Katherine Area Headquarters. On 22nd March 1942, Katherine sustained its only air raid during World War 11. One man was killed when a Japanese aircraft bombed the town. At that time vegetables were grown along the river for troop supplies. The wartime urgency formed the basis for experimentation in cropping along the riverbed. The town serves many cattle stations and farms growing sorghum, other cereal crops, and mangoes and receives produce from as far away as Wyndham, 480 kilometres west in Western Australia, to which it is connected by road. Some gold was found in the upper reaches of the Katherine River.

We boarded the boat, which took us down the Katherine River where large rock formations of the Gorge loomed over the calm water. The sounds of cicadas reverberate across the water between the imposing red ochre cliffs while you cruise down the first and second gorges listening to stories by the

Jawoyn people about how the Gorge was named. Nitmiluk is the Jawoyn name for Katherine Gorge. It is pronounced Nit-me-look, and literally means Cicada Place. The name was given by Nabilil, an important figure of the Creation Time. As he travelled through the country he came to the Gorge where he hears the song of the Cicada. "Nit, Nit, Nit"! The Nitmiluk National Park and Jawony Association logo is a painting by a deceased traditional owner of Nitmiluk. It depicts Bolung (the rainbow serpent), Nitmi (the Cicada), mussels, fish, and rocks. By tradition, Bolung still inhabits the deep pools of the second Gorge at Nitmiluk and care must be taken not to disturb him. Unlike other Jawoyn figures which may be addressed for assistance in hunting and foraging such a Barrava (Kookaburra), Bolung must not be spoken to. He is not only an important life giving figure but may also act as a destroyer. Today the Jawoyn people invite you to visit their country and to share the experience and magnificence of Nitmiluk Gorge. In the paintings in rock shelters, is the figure of the mythical 'Bula', the creator, who travelled this land.

The Gorge system is popular with visitors who go boating, canoeing and even swimming – for the very brave. Ranger Mr. McPhee said all visitors should be paying attention to the usual croc-wise message: "they're around, they can see you, you can't see them, so it's just safety on the banks and river edges at all times". Mr. McPhee said that the entire gorge system was closed for the wet season, as part of the crocodile management plan. "Part of our crocodile management plan is we will maintain one trap at the boat ramp in the first gorge by keeping it open, keeping it baited", he said. "We're just ready for 'em at any time, and if we can clear them out now it's not going to stop any more coming in the meantime" (McPhee, (2017, para. 9), states that...."we're ready for 'em at any time...."). He goes on to say, "at this time of the year, it's the crocodiles' domain; they can come and go as they please, we can't stop them". In the early days there were records of attacks because culling was in place, and the local crocodile population almost reached extinction. It took about 20 years before a "saltie" was seen in the Katherine River and that effectively executed the management plan. "But that does not mean there have been close calls", ranger Burke said. "Occasionally we heave reports that people have had a croc come up near the boat and have a snort". Crocodile numbers have expanded since culling was banned, and it is estimated that there are more than 100,000 in the Top End. Ranger Burke went on to say, "crocodiles can walk and if it is shallow or rocky it is still a danger" (Burke, (2019, para. 13), states that…."crocodiles can walk..".

From Katherine you can explore the Kakadu National Park by hiring a 4wd vehicle. Covering nearly 20,000 square kilometres, Kakadu National Park is a World Heritage Centre, renowned for both its cultural and natural values. It will take you about three hours to drive from Katherine along the Stuart Highway. I took a scenic flight over Kakadu which takes in views over the Arnhem Land escarpment, vast flood plains and billabongs. Wow, this was the best activity I did in the Northern Territory. But the Yellow River Cruise was excellent as well, the crocodiles (beware!) and bird life were a plenty, and the helicopter flight over the 13 gorges at Katherine was just amazing. I suggest that you spend time exploring Kakadu's other major Aboriginal rock art site – Nourlangie (Burrunggui), while a guide can provide a glimpse into how the local Aboriginal and Torres Strait Islander people lived. The Jumping Crocodile Cruise is one of the most popular tour destinations in the Northern Territory. Crocodiles along the river have learned to jump out of the water to snare small pieces of meat dangled from lines – great photo opportunity because you get a close up view of these aggressive creatures in the wild. Stop and visit the historic gold-mining centre of Pine Creek and have a quick dip at Maguk or Gunlom Falls.

Kakadu National Park was declared in stages, starting in the 1970's. Australians were becoming more interested in declaring national parks for conservation and in recognizing the land interest of Aboriginal people. The name Kakadu was suggested to recognize Gagudju, an Aboriginal language which used to be spoken in the park. A new area of woodland, called Koongarra (Kunkarra), was added to Kakadu National Park. Koongarra, which for more than a decade, Jeffrey Lee fought to prevent mining, lies in the shadow of Burrungkuy (nourlangie) rock – if you temporarily stop at the lookout to marvel at the view, you see Koongarra. On its other side, Koongarra faces Lightning Dreaming, home of Namarrkon or Lightning Man, the creation ancestor responsible for the dramatic electrical storms on the Arnhem plateau.

You can fly to Uluru (formerly Ayres Rock) from Alice Springs in about 50 minutes. Make the effort to go and watch the first rays of the sunset Uluru and the Red Centre illuminate – you won't regret it. The Uluru-Kata Tjuta National Park lies in the Red Centre and is home to many ancient wonders, the park is most famous for the enormous monoliths it's named after. Uluru and Kata Tjuta rise from the earth in all the scarlet magnificence just 30 kilometres from each other. The park, 1,325 square kilometres in size, is jointly managed by its traditional owners the Pitjantjatjara people, (who refer to themselves as Anangu people) and Parks Australia, and is in the spiritual heart of the Red Centre, about 450 kilometres southwest of Alice Springs by road. People from all over the world come to visit the World Heritage listed park, to wonder at its geological history, cultural significance and natural beauty. It is extremely difficult to accurately date the rock art at Uluru. Carbon dating can only pick up the age of the rock and the materials used for the pigments, rather than the paintings themselves. However, people are believed to have lived in the Uluru region for at least 30,000 years. Some paintings are considered to be 5000 years old. The Anangu traditionally made their paints from natural minerals and ash. The dry materials were placed on flat stones, crushed and mixed with kapi (water) or animal fat. The most common paint colours are red, yellow, orange, white, grey and black.

One terrific thing to do is to attend the Uluru Camel Cup. It is two days of outback entertainment when you join the locals for the weekend activities and experience a true Aussie outback style event. The 1oacclaimed Uluru Camel Cup Race Day begins with qualifying races on a 350 metre circular track, followed by an exciting Quarter Mile Flyer, Plate Race and the Uluru Camel Cup itself. There's plenty to see an do apart from the race – helicopter flights, outback games, whip cracking, fashions on the field, reptile show and food trucks. Race day is no doubt a bizarre one for the camels as well. The farm is home to 60 camels who spend their days plodding calmly through sand dunes, taking tourists on short walks that showcase views of Uluru and Kata Tjuta. The dust flies at the Cup, with five nail biting qualifying races followed by a Dash for Cash race. I did frock up for the races, however, did not partake in the Fashions on the Field parade. The weekend concluded with a true blue Frock Up and Rock Up Gala Ball set under the sparkling outback night sky, complete with a red desert dance floor, live entertainment and appetizing food. Each year the Uluru Camel Racing Club donates part proceeds to a charity.

When I recovered from the excitement of the Uluru Camel Cup, I joined a tour to the mystical domes of Kata Tjuta, formerly The Olgas, which is the name given to it thanks to the tallest peak, Mount Olga, which juts out a little higher than the other rock formations in the vicinity. Mount Olga, rising 546 metres above ground level, was named by

Ernest Giles back in 1872 after Queen Olga of Wurttemberg, daughter of Tsar Nicholas 1. She married Karl of Wurttemberg who, as it turned out, was homosexual so Olga had no children. With no children of her own, Olga dedicated her life to social causes. Together with Uluru, this collection of large domed rock formations, they make up the two most popular landmarks in the Uluru-Kata Tjuta National Park, is considered to be a sacred site to the Aboriginal people of Australia. It is recognized by UNESCO as a World Heritage Area for both its natural and cultural values. Kata Tjuta is a Pitjantjatjara term that means "many heads" (Uluru-Kata Tjuta National Park, (ND. para. 1) states that…."Kata-Tjuta means 'many heads"). It is hallowed to the local Aboriginal Anangu people, who have inhabited the area for more than 22,000 years. I joined a cultural tour to learn some of the region's sacred history and fascinating Dreamtime stories. There are a few legends that remember the great snake king, Wanambi, who was thought to reside at the top of Mount Olga, only coming down to ground level in the dry season. Legend has it that his breath could turn a breeze into a hurricane, punishing those who committed evil deeds in the region. There is no such a stunning experience as the sunset at Kata Tjuta and you bring your dinner and ponder the domes changing from pink to deep red as the sun goes down.

I recommend that if you're going out to the Red Centre, you must not miss out on the Olgas and their importance to the community.

Jim Jim Falls is and iconic part of Kakadu famous for its amazing cliffs and thundering waterfalls. In the dry season the falls stop running and you can hike into the heart of the gorge and sit in the shadow of these grand and dramatic cliffs. The waterfalls are best seen by air during the tropical summer, m when heavy rains send huge volumes of water crashing into the gorge below. With the peace and serenity of this special place, you should take your time to connect with the Indigenous culture.

Katherine Telegraph Station was established on 22nd August 1872 and the completion of the Overland Telegraph Line later in 1872, and the town began with a small permanent population on the west side of the Katherine River. The Northern Australia Railway was extended to Katherine with construction beginning in 1923 of the Katherine railway bridge. The original post office and the Overland Telegraph Station were set just above Knott's Crossing and next to the Sportsman's Arms Hotel that had quarters for the station master at the Overland Telegraph Station and a single room police station.

In April 2006 floods placed parts of the town under water, including about 50 houses, and caused millions of dollars of damage. Residents had time to escape with little more than the clothes they were wearing. On Australia Day in 1998 a major flood resulted from the 300-400 mm of rainwater brought by Cyclone Les that caused the already full Katherine River to peak at 20.4 metres. The floodwaters inundated the town and much of the surrounding region, requiring the evacuation of many residents. Three people drowned.

Tom Curtain's Katherine Outback Experience (he is a multiple Golden Guitar winner) celebrates the Northern Territory's unique Pastoral history and culture through real horse-starting and working dog demonstrations, live music and story telling. This is not your average type of outback show or tour, rather it is an adventure! It is frank and realistic, the same as if an audience wasn't present. This hands-on experience is located on an operating farm, just 6 kilometres south of Katherine. Guests are seated on comfortable benches under the shade of an indoor arena, and watch and learn as the young horses and working dogs are trained for working life on the land. Training is achieved from a relationship built on trust. Guests are invited to pat and feed the station animals including the horses, dogs, buffalo, cattle and goats to name a few.

We finally arrive in Darwin. The Ghan's arrival in Darwin signified the beginning of a new and distinctive period of tourism in the Northern Territory, making travel to the region easier and more convenient as well as providing better access to and for Aboriginal communities in the region. With a 2018 estimated population of 148,564, it has more residents than the rest of the sparsely populated Northern Territory. I stayed at the Darwin City Hotel in the heart of Darwin, just 10 minutes walk to the The Esplanade and Parliament House. I loved my stay there – great amenities, fantastic food and the staff were lovely and friendly.

Darwin City History has been written in sudden large steps rather than having moved slowly. The Tennant Creek gold rush in 1933 provided another surge for Darwin as men and equipment travelled to the goldfields. Gold did strange things to men and the mining rush that followed set something of a precedent for the way Darwin has developed.

From there, the people of Darwin with much enthusiasm elected a local government, and on July 1 2007, Darwin commemorated its 50th anniversary since self-governance with birthday celebrations and the placing of a time capsule in Darwin's Civic Park.

The Darwin region, like much of the Top End, experiences a tropical climate with a wet and dry season. A period known locally as "the build up" leading up to Darwin's wet season see temperatures and humidity increase. The wet season (November to April) typically arrives in late November to early December and brings with it heavy monsoonal downpours, spectacular lightning displays and increased cyclone activity. The best time is in the dry season (May to October) when the city has clear skies and mild sea breezes from the harbour.

The biggest change was delivered in a few hours by Cyclone Tracey in 1974 in the early hours of Christmas Day. Cyclone Tracy devastated the city, nearly completely destroying it. 66 people were killed (mostly stuck by flying debris) and thousands more were injured. More than 30,000 of the then population were evacuated to cities and towns all over Australia immediately after the devastation. Many returned to resume their lives, and the Reconstruction Commission, made up of Federal, Territory, and Local Government representatives began to run and rebuild the city which gradually turned Darwin into the most modern capital city in Australia. Many of the victims of the cyclone are buried at the Darwin General Cemetery. The rebuilding that followed has left a dwell-designed, modern city with very few old buildings. The Fannie Bay Gaol is one of the few buildings in Darwin that survived the winds of Cyclone Tracey.

Queensland and Northern Territory Air Services Aviation has played a significant part in Darwin's history. Ross and Keith Smith landed here to achieve the first flight from England to Australia in 1919. Early planes battled with the distance from Europe, and Darwin became a vital stopover airport. A visit to the original Qantas hangar at the site or the original Darwin Civil Aerodrome is well worth it. Originally part of South Australia, the Northern territory was separated from South Australia and transferred to Commonwealth control on 1st January 1911. In 1918, unpopular decisions about the price of beer and other critical issues by the Administrator John Gilruth led to a strong protest movement known as The Darwin Rebellion.

The traditional owners of Darwin are the Larrakia (saltwater) people. Larrakia country runs far beyond the municipal boundaries of Darwin, covering the area from the Cox peninsula in the west to the Adelaide River in the east. The Larrakia people established the first trade routes in the region, trading with the Tiwi, Wagait, and Wulna people, as well as with Indonesian fishermen. Complex and fascinating in equal measure, the Aboriginal history of Darwin and the Tiwi Islands dates back tens of thousands of years. You can get an overview at the Museum and Art Gallery of the Northern Territory or delve deeper with a living history lesson and guided tour from the land's traditional owners. The Larrakia people have a deep, spiritual connection to the land, and are taking responsibility to ensure the land is respected by all those that use it. The Australian Aboriginal people are an ancient civilization, as they have inhabited the country for over 65,000 years, occupying the country well before European invasion in the 1800s. The Larrakia community had a strong connection to the sea, hunting the waters for their food. They had a close relationship with the neighbouring tribes, trading their food, shared ceremonies and allow marriage within the neighbouring groups. They were introduced to the settlement life, living in and around the city, before being moved out to outer camp areas. The Aboriginal people were grossly mistreated by Europeans, and the invasion caused a catastrophic destruction of the community which is still felt today. Despite this, the Larrakia people are still a strong and vibrant community. They are renowned for their skills in art, music and governmental positions. You can immerse yourself in the compelling history of the Top End, where everyone has a story: Aboriginal Dreamtime stories, tales of pioneering spirit and immigration, survival stories of WW11 and Cyclone Tracey. From any perspective, the region's history is fascinating.

Due to the remote location of Darwin, Europeans did not settle in this area until the country's infrastructure made it possible. In 1839, the HMS Beagle with Lt. John Stokes aboard sailed into the waters of what is now known as Darwin harbour. Stokes named the harbour after his former shipmate British evolutionist Charles Darwin, but contrary to popular rumours, Darwin himself never visited the area. The crew members of an English ship, named the HMS Beagle, were the first European settlers to spot Darwin. John Clements Wickham, the captain of the ship, named the area "Port Darwin" after the former shipmate Charles Darwin, who had sailed on the ship's previous voyage. The final name change was in 1911, changing the official area "Darwin". Darwin was originally called Palmerston, although the port was always known as Port Darwin. The discovery of gold at Pine Creek in 1871, accelerated the growth of the town, and the young settlement was renamed Darwin, and was granted city status in 1959.

The period between 1911 and 1919 was filled with political disorder, particularly with trade union unrest, which concluded on the 17th December 1918. Led by Harold Nelson, some 1000 demonstrators marched to Government House Liberty Square in Darwin where they burned an effigy of the Administrator of the Northern Territory, John Gilruth and demanded his resignation. The incident became known as the Darwin Rebellion. Their grievances were against the two main Northern Territory employers; Vestey's Meatworks and the Federal Government. Both Gilruth and the Vestey company left Darwin soon afterwards. In early 1875 Darwin's white population had grown to approximately 300 because of the gold rush. On the 17th February 1875, the SS Gothenburg left Darwin en route for Adelaide. The approximately 88 passengers and 34 crew included Government officials, circuit-court judges, Darwin residents taking their first holiday, and miners.

The Dutch visited the northern coastline in the 1600s and landed on the Tiwi Islands only to be thwarted by the Tiwi people. The Dutch, however, created the first European maps of the area, hence the Dutch names, such as Arnhem Land and Groote Eylandt.

At the beginning of World War 11 Darwin only had a population of 2000 and was extremely isolated with a small airport, unsealed roads to the rest of Australia and little infrastructure.

During World War 11, Darwin and many other towns and communities were extensively bombed. Between February 1942 and October 1943, there were more than 60 air raids over Darwin, killing more than 243 people and destroyed many public buildings, including the post office, where 9 people perished after a direct hit on the bomb shelter. Eight allied ships were sunk in Darwin Harbour and 24 allied aircraft were destroyed, along with an air raid on the Darwin RAAF base. The bombing of Darwin has had a lasting effect on the City, both in the destruction caused and massive build up of the area by allied forces. To aid the war effort, the road to Alice Springs was upgraded and sealed, large military airports were built at Darwin and Batchelor and many smaller airfields were built. The Adelaide River developed as an important strategic military base with ammunition dumps, supply depots and a hospital. The railway was strengthened to handle a massive increase in traffic and the rail bridge was decked to provide a wet season crossing for road traffic. Darwin's pioneering and pre-war history endures in the city's surviving buildings: visit the early pioneers' stone buildings – Browns Mart, Government House and the Fannie Bay Gaol – before moving on to pre-war psycho architecture and high tea at Burnett House.

Through the 60s and 70s Darwin continued to grow steadily, but was still very isolated with roads into the town cut frequently during the tropical wet season.

In the 1870s, relatively large numbers of Chinese settled at least temporarily in the Northern Territory; many were contracted to work the goldfields and later to build the Palmerston to Pine Creek railway. By 1888 there were 6122 Chinese in the Northern Territory, mostly in or around Darwin. The early Chinese settlers were mainly from Guangdong Province in south China. However, at the end of the nineteenth century anti-Chinese feelings grew in response to the 1890s economic depression, and the White Australia Policy meant many Chinese left the area and returned to China. But some families stayed, became Australian citizens and established a commercial base in Darwin.

Today, Darwin is a cosmopolitan city, with the Chinese Temple and Museum Chung Wah being one of the focal points of the community. The museum documents the history of the Chinese population of the Territory over more than a century, and the beautiful temple (originally built in 1887) is used daily as a place of worship. It's especially exciting to visit the temple during events, and during Chinese New Year you'll also see lion dancers around the city as they bless more than 400 businesses and homes.

Darwin is a city with a distinctive blend of cultures and is the final stop on the Ghan. Darwin's nearness to Indonesia has created a melting pot of food, culture and colours. An example of Darwin's cultural diversity, is the Mindil Beach Sunset Markets. Twice a week Mindil Beach is transformed into a market place full of food, clothing and interesting trinkets. In other words, you can eat your way around the world. Mindil Beach is strikingly beautiful and definitely merits a visit in its own right.

Aviation played a significant part in Darwin's history. Ross and Keith Smith landed there to achieve the first flight from England to Australia in 1919. As early planes struggled with the distance from Europe, Darwin became a vital stopover airport.

Travelling and sight-seeing can be exhausting, so the Douglas Hot Springs are a fantastic way to relax, unwind and restore yourself so that you can get ready to see more of Darwin and surrounds.

A fascinating place to visit are the Tiwi Islands, which are a chain of nine islands 80 kilometres north of Darwin, and two of the largest are inhabited. The vast majority of residents of these two islands are the Tiwi people, and Indigenous Australian people who are believed to have lived there for at least 7,000 years; they are also the first Indigenous peoples to have made historically recorded contact with Europeans (Dutch explorers, in the early 18th Century). I boarded the ferry which takes 2.5 hours from Darwin to the island. You can also fly there in 30 minutes. As the boat slided onto the beach, we were greeted first by Claudia, the crocodile who likes to chill in the blue-green waters in front of the retreat. Although she is small, she is noisy and is always on site – even if you can't see her, watching her do her vanishing act is gripping.

Often referred to as the Islands of Smiles, the Tiwi Island Retreat, which is in one of the most remote parts of the planet, is a wonderful place to visit and enjoys a strong and vivid Indigenous history and culture, with a thriving local art scene that is an important part of both the culture and economy of the Tiwi Islands, and with enchanting myths and stories that play a major part in shaping their communities. A wonderful spot for nature lovers and bird-watchers as well, it is the home of gorgeous varied lorikeets, northern rosellas, the sea turtles and many other magnificent bird species. Strictly speaking, there aren't many tourist attractions on the island as such, but that's part of the pleasure of this off-the-beaten-track part of Australia: you're visiting an area of natural beauty and welcoming locals. Staying at the Tiwi Island Retreat was a truly memorable experience and it's where I could get away from the crowds and experience the unique, unspoiled environment, activities and culture.

The Tiwi Island Retreat was originally established as a barramundi fishing lodge, and the rooms, which once were set up for fishing enthusiasts, have now been refurbished into beautiful and simple coastal style rooms with crisp linen, towels, and air-conditioning. From relaxing by the pool to amazing outback adventures, world renowned fishing and Indigenous art and educational tours offer something for everyone. I don't know whether it's the remoteness, or maybe it's beauty you can soak in as you perhaps sip a drink on one of the verandahs and watch that sun sink behind Claudia's playground. This place promotes sociability. You can chat to most of the guests and the staff during your stay. It's not unusual for a hungry crocodile to check out the odd crab pot up here, so it's just as well Dwayne skippers our boat when we headed out. There is sudden inspiration as he hauled up each pot to reveal small crabs, which are thrown back when larger ones are caught. The fishing can be hair-raising, and when one of us hauled in a huge cod, we were all relieved it didn't turn out to be something even bigger! Later we went out with Dwayne again, this time in a beach buggy on terra firma for a sunset picnic further up the deserted beach where Dwayne built and lighted a camp fire to sit by, complete with cheese platter and champagne. When we presented our huge cod and mud crabs to Siggy the chef and all-round problem solver, she knew exactly what to do; the cod was not the best for grilling – we had fresh barramundi for that. Instead she served juicy fat "fish bites" done in a light, crispy batter to accompany our cooked crab legs, grilled barra, tangy salad, thick-cut chips and ice-cold beers and white wine.

The food was confirmation to Siggy's creativity and cooking skills; there are no local shops so she needed to plan tactically and wasted nothing.

So, her distress is understood when, for example, the boat arrives without the pumpkin she ordered for her ravioli and she hastily changes the menu. Notwithstanding the difficulties, the food here is unbelievably fresh and tasty and makes good use of all that tropical produce just a plane flight away. The wild beauty of this place is priceless – luxury is not always a private spa bath and a big television. I'LL BE BACK.

For the courageous ones, you can get up close and personal with the fearsome crocodiles which are quite an icon of the Northern Territory, especially when you hear about people (like Prince Harry for example) wrestling them! The Northern Territory is the first place that would come to mind for most Australians, when crocodiles are mentioned, as well as anyone who saw the movie Crocodile Dundee. Crocosaurus Cove offers the timorous Cage of Death experience, where the only thing keeping you from becoming crocodile food is the cage you're inside of as it is lowered into croc-infested waters; a video of the Cage posted to a Facebook page has been viewed over 30 million times since being posted in October 2016, to the thrill of the friendly staff at Croc Cove. It is fun feeding the baby crocs and watching the big ones being fed by the trainers. The staff and the animals are well looked after. More family-friendly and less terrifying, is Crocodylus Park, where you can get to know Darwin's favourite massive reptile, with over a thousand crocs in the Park. Hundreds too many for me! But it is quite safe with many security personnel on hand.

Have a look at the massive termite mounds of which you'll find hundreds of huge termite-built structures measuring up to two metres high and complete with nursery chambers, tunnels, chimneys and more. There's termite mounds in every continent of the world, but only Australia has these "magnetic" mounds, named as such because they tend to align in a north-to-south direction. Astonishing!

The Arafura Games is a unique and inclusive multi-sport 6event where athletes with a disability compete in the same program as able-bodied athletes. This week-long event is held every 2 years in Darwin, and attracts competitors from around the world. I was lucky enough to be there at that time and was able to attend. If you go to this event, you will take home some of the most memorable experiences ever. The Arafura Games takes its name from the Arafura Sea, which lies between the Northern Territory and Southeast Asia. The name Arafura is from the Indigenous name for "the people of mountains" (Wikipedia, (ND. para. 3) states that…."Hampton means 'place near rocks in the river'), and is a shallow sea in the western Pacific ocean, spanning 650,000 square kilometres between the Gulf of Carpentaria and the south coast of New Guinea. Nations around the Arafura Sea originally took part, however, in recent years countries from further afield have participated, including the United States, England and Brazil, to name just a few.

The 90 musicians strong Darwin Symphony Orchestra, which performs all over the Northern Territory, is the Territory's most important cultural institution. The Orchestra has performed concerts in places such as Katherine, Tennant Creek, Alice Springs, Glen Helen Gorge, Groote Eylandt, Nhulunbuy and Jabiru. The DSO was twice presented with the National Australia Day Community Event of the Year Award. In 1995 the DSO received the award for Outstanding Contribution to Australian Culture from the Centre of Australian Cultural Research. In 2000 the Orchestra was presented by the Orchestras of Australia Network with the award for a community orchestra.

The Museum and Art Gallery of the Northern Territory is the Northern Territory's premier cultural institution. Permanent exhibition highlights include, Cyclone Tracy, Natural History and Sweetheart the crocodile, as well as temporary exhibitions.

Sweetheart (this name caused confusion over his gender) a large male saltwater (Estaurine) crocodile, is a celebrated identity of recent Northern Territory history. In the 1970's, Sweetheart gained notoriety for attacking dinghies at popular Darwin fishing spots. Then in early 1979, the attacks became more frequent, and safety concerns were raised. The Parks and Wildlife Commission decided to capture Sweetheart and relocate him to a local crocodile farm. Sweetheart was caught in a trap and anaesthetized, but in the attempt to haul this monstrous animal ashore, he became entangled with a sunken log and drowned. The body can be seen in the Museum and Art Gallery where the taxidermist has prepared Sweetheart as a skin mount. Although a large mature male, Sweetheart is not the largest crocodile known. Estaurine (or Saltwater) crocodiles are distributed throughout India, South-east Asia, Papua New Guinea and islands of the Western Pacific, as well as northern Australia, and specimens exceeding 6 metres in length have been recorded.

In true Northern Territory spirit, the Darwin Beer Can Regatta is a festival held annually since 1974 at Mindil Beach. Participants create boats using empty beer cans, soft drink cans, soft drink bottles and milk cartons. Up to 30,000 cans have been used for a single boat. Various events take place with the regatta, including concerts, sandcastles, a thong-throwing contest, the best novelty hat and the "Henley-on-Mindil" competition (named after the Henley-on-Todd Regatta), where participants run their "boats" around like Flinstones cars. The 2014 Darwin Lions Beer Can Regatta took place on 6th July, 2014 when it was watched by 15,000 people and attended by visitors from all over Australia. The winner of the first beer can regatta was Kevin Jaques driving the Darwin's Powerboat Club's entry "Pistol Knight". Because Kevin used only Swan beer cans, he was presented with the doubled winning cheques totalling $1000, by the Sales Manager for Swan Brewery, Des Hoare!

Get the best guaranteed sunset vista by cruising across Darwin Harbour on a large, ocean-going catamaran with plenty of deck space. You can sit under the sails or in the air-conditioned salon and toast the incredible setting sun with a glass of sparkling wine and a tapas/barbeque dinner. You can take another sunset cruise aboard the "Charles Darwin" deluxe 3-level catamaran and hear live commentary on Darwin's history and landmarks and have the option to include a buffet dinner, or purchase sack and drinks at the onboard bar. A visit to the Darwin Military Museum, is a worthwhile history lesson. I found the entire complex interesting, from the short film of the bombing through to the static and interactive displays. It has a wonderful display of WW 11 artefacts. During the war, Darwin was bombed 64 times over almost two years, with first two raids alone resulted in the deaths of an estimated 243 people. However, other sources place the figure as much higher, even up to 1000. The memorial plaque on the Darwin Esplanade overlooking the harbour says 292 people were killed. Since then the Darwin City Council commissioned naval historian John Bradford to determine the truth on how many died. One for the bucket list? Yes!

The hop-on and hop-off open-top double-decker bus provides unobstructed views and an informative onboard commentary.

If you like casinos, poker machines, world-class restaurants, elegant bars, and resort accommodation, then you can enjoy the charm and glamour of the Darwin Casino. Darwin Casino is one of the renowned Skycity chain of casinos; it was the second casino to ever open in Australia, and is the only casino in Darwin. The interior is well furnished and equipped. Even if you're not into gambling, it's fun to wander around the resort and immerse yourself in the beautiful setting and the plush atmosphere.

For the energetic ones, you can wakeboard, or waterski at the Darwin Ski Club, where you can watch the sun set over the harbour while enjoying a drink and dinner.

I highly recommend Darwin's Deckchair Cinema for its great vibes and incredible sunset views, not to mention the warm welcome. This grand open air cinema is situated on the gorgeous Darwin Harbour, screening various Australian, foreign, popular, classic and family friendly films. You can enjoy dinner, drinks and snacks from the fully licensed kiosk, or you can bring a picnic. A fabulous experience with comfy chairs and cushions in an amazing location, amongst tropical surrounds.

I enjoyed my stay in Darwin – you need at least a week to get to see most attractions. From Darwin I went to Broome, famous for pearls and took a tour around the north west to Cape Leveque, Fitzroy Crossing, Halls Creek and Kununurra in the Bungles Bungles Range. On another trip I went on a coach tour down the Western Australian coast from Darwin to Perth, stopping at Port Hedland, 80 mile beach, the longest beach in Australia – 220 kilometres forming the coastline where the Great Sandy Desert approaches the Indian Ocean, Exmouth, Coral Bay, Monkey Mia, Kalbarri, the Pinacles and New Norcia. Spent some time in Perth and then, you guessed it, boarded the Indian Pacific to Sydney.

CHAPTER 8

Queensland Rail Tales

nd now for Queensland Rail. There's no better way to skip the hassles of traffic or stretching necks for a glimpse through the clouds on a plane, and instead view this beautiful part of the world from just outside the window of your long-distance train. Queensland has a distinctive spirit, thanks to a lush coastline brimming with flora and fauna, delicious produce, relaxed locals and adventures aplenty.

I convinced my dear and long-time friend Judy Ley to come with me on a rail escapade in Queensland. I had heard such good reports that I was determined to explore Queensland by rail.

We set off on the XPT to Brisbane, arriving early the next morning. We were met by friends Jean and Irene and spent most of the day with them, sightseeing and lunching before we checked in at our hotel for a three day stay.

Brisbane is the most populous city of Queensland and has a population of 2.6 million. It is situated within the peninsular of the Brisbane River about from its mouth at Moreton Bay. The colloquial name for Brisbane people is "Brisbanite", while common nicknames for the city include "Brissie" and the "River City. Brisbane was founded upon the traditional lands of the Turrbal people, whose name for the area on which the city is located is Meanjin. The Turrbal Tribe includes direct descendants of the original owners and custodians of Brisbane. These bloodlines connect Turrbal peoples' past, present and future to one another, with traditional customs and laws intact. The beautiful ancestral homelands of the Turrbal Tribe stretch north from Elimbah Creek, south to the Logan River, and inland as far as Moggill. They are dedicated to ensuring the survival and continuous sharing of the Turrbal culture and traditions, to developing self-sustaining communities and that Indigenous and non-Indigenous people will be able to celebrate the rich culture and history of the Turrbal Tribe. We attended the Spirits of the Red Sand genre-defying cultural theatre show, which is like nothing both of us have experienced before. Based on true Aboriginal and Colonial events that occurred at the turn of the twentieth century, this was a captivating and passionately raw piece of theatre that deals with serious themes in a sensitive yet steadfast way. In prime position on the Brisbane River and opposite the CBD is Brisbane's lively hub, South Bank. Parks, gardens, galleries, restaurants, cafes and even a man made beach bring this precinct to life, which roused our days of discovery from our first cappuccino through to the cocktail hour. South Bank is a central stop on the CityCat ferry route, so our journey there doubled as a scenic river cruise. Gliding along the Brisbane River is a great way to get your bearings of the city as you take in the views of the kayakers and rock climbers making the most of Brisbane's year-round outdoor lifestyle. So, we joined in. No matter that hour of the day you visit, you'll find New Farm and Fortitude Valley in fine fettle, New Farm and Fortitude Valley has been strongly influenced by urban renewal, so today the duo are two of Brisbane's most popular destinations, tempting visitors from near and far with their many activities for both day and night. A venturer's dream just 75 minutes by ferry from Brisbane, Moreton, the third-largest sand island in the world, is a natural wonder. The Island consists entirely of sand, apart from a small area of sandstone and rhyolite at Cape Moreton, which has built up over the past 400,000 years. It is also home to the highest coastal sand dune in the world, Mount Tempest, which at 285 metres provides 360 degrees of stunning views.

Brisbane was first seen by Europeans in the 1600s, when Dutch explorer Willam Jansz landed on the Cape York Peninsula in 1606, and in 1623 Jan Carstens explored the Gulf of Carpentaria. An Englishman, Lieutenant James Cook, is acknowledged as the first European to encounter Queensland's east coast in 1770 in HMS Endeavour. Europeans settled in Queensland in 1825 when Brisbane was selected as a penal settlement for more difficult convicts. The penal settlement was officially closed in 1839 and the land was prepared for sale for permanent settlement.

Queensland was originally part of the British-administered colony of New South Wales, which occupied a large part of the Australian continent. A desire to separate from New South Wales began to emerge as Queensland's economic significance increased and its productivity and population expanded. The people of Queensland began to realise the importance of Brisbane as a port and urban centre. In 1851, a public meeting was held to consider Queensland's separation. Queen Victoria granted approval and signed Letters Patent in 1859 to establish the new colony of Queensland.

In the same year, an Order-in-Council gave Queensland its own constitution, and Queensland became a self-governing colony with its own Governor, a nominated Legislative Council and an elected Legislative Assembly. Queensland Day is celebrated on 6th June, recognizing the birth of the state. After the separation from New South Wales towns outside Brisbane began to develop, and in 1860 Ipswich and Rockhampton were officially declared towns. Maryborough and Warwick followed in the next year. Queensland's first elections were held in 1860, and Robert George Wyndham led the first elected Government as Premier. One of the earliest decisions of the new parliament was to increase the population of the new colony as rapidly as possible. The discovery of payable gold near Rockhampton was one of the many discoveries that encouraged development in Queensland and helped to protect the state from the effects of the 1866 Depression. By 1891, wool had become an enormous industry in Australia. Thousands of shearers, already dissatisfied with their pay rates and conditions, refused to work when a Darling Downs Station employed non-union immigrants began working for even cheaper wages, the potential for revolution dissolved. The strike is remembered as an event that created camaraderie among Australian workers from all backgrounds and launched Labor politics. The first branch meeting of the Australian Labor Party is said to have been held by striking shearers under the gum tree now known as the Tree of Knowledge in Barcaldine.

As fears were expressed that Aboriginal people in Queensland faced extinction, the Government decided to establish new governmental reserves to accommodate the remaining tribes throughout the state. In 1897, the Aboriginal Protection and Restriction of the Sale of Opium Act was passed, authorizing the removal of Aboriginal people to reserves. These of removal continued until 1971 when the

Act was amended. In 1901, the union of the Commonwealth of Australia was created. The majority of Queenslanders voted yes to a referendum asking whether Queensland should join the Federation. The referendum was passed resulting in Queensland losing its colonial status and becoming a state.

A diverse city with 32,2% of its metropolitan population being foreign-born, Brisbane is classified as a global city and ranks highly in ratings of liveable cities. The city is named after the Brisbane River on which it stands, and in turn named after Sir Thomas Brisbane, the governor of New South Wales at the time of the city's founding. Brisbane is known for its distinct Queensland architecture – the archetypal Queenslander is a single detached house made of timber with a corrugated iron roof located on a separate block of land. They are all high-set, single-storey dwellings which provides air flow needed in the warm climate, and with a characteristic veranda that extends around the house to varying lengths but never entirely surrounds it. In later years many have been renovated to enclose part of all of these verandas to create extra bedrooms. The underneath of the house is often also enclosed to provide extra living areas, which leads to the common misconception that an authentic Queenslander has two storeys. Amidst the shyscrapers sits an open-air city that embraces the river at its heart. We sampled the culinary delights offered by amazing chefs in a growing army of first class restaurants and hotels.

Moreton Bay and its islands are referred to as Quandamooka, which includes the Ngugi tribe on Moreton Island and the Gorenpul and Nunukil clans on North Stradbroke island. The Aboriginal name for Moreton Island is Mulgumpin meaning "place of sandhills". For 50,000 years the Australian Aborigines relied and plants and animals for food, medicines, shelter, tools and clothing. The Ngugi people, who connected with the land and sea have strong spiritual basis and some animals are strongly linked with traditions and customs. The Ngugi people who lived on Moreton Island for over 2,000 years, relied heavily on resources from the sea, fish, shellfish, dugong and turtle making up a major portion their diet. On the 31st July, Matthew Flinders discovered that the land south of Cape Moreton was in fact an island and named it Moreton Island following Captain Cook's trend. In January 1823, ticket-of-leave convicts, Pamphlett, Parsons and Finnegan, left Sydney to fell timber at Illawarra. They were caught in a storm, blown north and after 21 days at sea with very little water, desperate and near death, managed to beach their boat on Moreton Island. With the help of local Aborigines, they recovered sufficiently to make their way to the southern end of the island via the western beach and were transported to Stradbroke Island in a canoe. They were treated kindly by the Aboriginal people for their stay of a week or ten days and accommodated in a large hut of their own and supplied with food, water and any other necessities.

The Cape Moreton iconic red and white banded Lighthouse is located on the Northern point of Moreton Island and was the first lighthouse to be built in Queensland. A lake on Moreton Island has found a new lease of life after a group of Chinese visitors to the Tangalooma Island Resort, which is also home to amazing natural flora and fauna, realized it resembled the shape of a wild dolphin. We had booked a day cruise on Tangalooma from Brisbane – we enjoyed out time on the island and we wished we could have stayed longer. A fantastic short break on this great Resort. The Champagne Pools on Moreton Island get their name from the sparkling 'champagne' effect generated as the ocean waves crash over the volcanic rock and sandstone break wall. A beautiful photo opportunity. The surfside of Moreton Island, otherwise known as Eastern Beach, contains six almost continuous beaches that stretch for around 27 kilometres in length.

Where else in the world are you going to find something like this? The Eastern side of Moreton Island is unprotected by land causing crashing waves popular with surfers. A lovely little sleepy town on the Southern end of Moreton Island, is Kooringal, where notable highlights include the Oyster Farm and Gutter Bay. Kooringal means 'home by the sea'. We did not have time, but, there was the Gheebulum Cooungai (Moreton Bay) National Park, the Moreton Bay Marine Park, Mirapool Lagoon, Harper's Rock, Honeymoon Bay (which I was told, looks something like a Hollywood movie set), Mount Tempest, the Princess Theatre and more to visit. Next time. Judy and I will be back.

First up, The Spirit of the Outback and the journey to Longreach. We departed Brisbane on a Tuesday in the early evening and arrived the next day at 7.20pm. What an easy way to travel the 1300 kilometres to Longreach and watch the beautiful scenic views go by while sitting in your sleeping berth. We each had a single sleeper (I snore) berth which featured all the mod cons, washbasin, wardrobe, vanity mirror, towels, sheets and blankets. Showers were positioned at the rear of the carriage. For first class customers meals were taken in the themed Tuckerbox Restaurant featuring Aussie meals or a selection of take away options for the Club Car. There is also an on board lounge, The Shearer's Rest, for drinks and chatting with new found friends. Because this is a gentle and luxurious way to travel it tends to suit older travellers. I was asked by a gentleman with a young son, why everyone appeared to be older, and he said, "because they had the money and the time to travel". The young boy said "No they have less time Dad". I guess there was some logic in there somewhere.

On our journey we passed Ipswich, Laidley and Toowoomba. Although the Spirit of the Outback doesn't stop at Toowoomba, the best way to get there is by coach 1 hour 45 minutes, and there are several carriers you can choose from. Toowoomba is described as the Garden City, and that description is accurate. It has some superb parks and elegant buildings, such as the Cobb & Co Museum. It is perched 600-800 metres above sea level on the edge of a plateau, and when I visited there previously, I made the climb up from the plains to the plateau. My ears popped like champagne and you could smell the peace up there. Picnic Point offers spectacular views and behind it the city seems to float down though the suburbs to the CBD. Nowhere else in Queensland would you experience all four seasons as characteristically as right here – crisp Winter air, knee-deep autumn leaves, clear summer days and a splash of colour in spring.

Prior to European settlement the escarpment was home to the Barunggam Aborigines. No one is quite sure what 'toowoomba" meant in the language of the local Barumggam people, but it has been claimed that 'toowoomba' means either 'the swamp, a variety of melon on the edge of the swamp. The confusion is caused because some experts argue that the name is a corruption of 'tchwampa' – the swamp, others say it is derived from 'choowoom' meaning native melon and others contend it comes from 'woomba woomba' meaning 'reeds in the swamp'. After squatter Thomas Alford settled to the north of Drayton and called his property "Toowoomba" that the name was eventually accepted. It was declared a city in 1904. The Indigenous population was devastated by diseases such as smallpox, influenza and measles brought by the settlers. These introduced diseases as well as social disruption, relocation and murder, caused the Indigenous population to be almost wiped out. In the local First Nations community, Toowoomba is known as a key meeting place along the ancient pathways that led to huge festivals at the Bunya Mountains, held every three years or so to celebrate the harvest of bunya nuts. The bunya nut tree is native to south-eastern Queensland, especially in the Bunya

Mountains National Park. It is a huge tree which bears a crop only after the tree itself is around 100 years old, and then it crops once every two or three years.

We sped past Chinchilla, Roma and Mitchell and finally arrived in Charleville. We travelled by coach to Winton, a journey of 2 hours, 10 minutes – ouch! However quite comfortable.

Winton is the Dinosaur Capital of Australia, the home of Banjo Patterson's Waltzing Matilda and the Boulder Opal; abundant in character, knowledge and heritage. Winton is situated on the Great Artesian Basin, one of the largest artesian groundwater basins in the world. One can learn all about Australia's adopted national anthem at the Waltzing Matilda Centre. The Waltzing Matilda Centre has a great historical display about the area of Winton as well as lots of information on the famous Banjo Paterson. Included in the Main Exhibition is the story of the renowned song through interactive displays. According to general belief, it was inspired by an 1894 shearer's suicide at the nearby Combo Waterhole and first performed in Winton's North Gregory Hotel on 6th April 1895, the first pub to hear the song. Unofficial Australian anthems aren't the only things that's put Winton on the map; this is dinosaur territory. The Australian Age of Dinosaurs Museum holds the world's largest collection Australian dinosaur fossils. It's a great visit for self-proclaimed dino-geeks or just those interested in all things history. Those who are employed at the museum go on special digs for fossils, so their collection has been increasing since they opened in Belmont. I opted to go on a Dig-a-Dino experience. It was the source of most enjoyment. The entire tour takes up seven days, but you'll only be digging for five or six of them. Included in the price ($3500 for new diggers), you'll get accommodation, all meals and pre-dinner drinks. You also get to take an excursion to the museum's laboratory, where you learn how fossils are studied. If you just want to help but don't have enough time to spend a whole week digging, the Prep-a-Dino (I love the terminology), experience is worth the short two-day journey. You can hop on board a shuttle bus tour to Dinosaur Canyon and see Australia's prehistoric landscape. You wouldn't guess it but there's only one site in the world that has evidence of a dinosaur stampede, and it is in Winton, Outback Queensland. In October 2016 a new species, Savannasaurus Elliottorum, was officially named, the fossilized skeleton of this 18 metre long dinosaur discovered by Winton grazier, David Elliott, on his property while mustering sheep. It wasn't the first time Elliott came across bones: that was back in 1999, and his family went on to establish the Australian Age of Dinosaur museum on their property, which now claims to be the largest collection of Australian dinosaur fossils in the world. In the late 1970s, scientists found fossils and footprints in the surrounding areas in Lark Quarry, believing that millions of years ago, there was a stampede of over 150 two-legged dinosaurs. During this time Lark Quarry was excavated and became an Environmental Park. You can only see it from afar due to the safety of preserving this splendid piece of land.

764.6 kilometres from Winton is Riversleigh comprising (10,000 hectacres) of the southern section of Lawn Hill (Boodjamulla) National park in north-west Queensland. Riversleigh was declared a World Heritage site in 1994 because of the quality of fossils it yields. Fossil fauna from the Riversleigh site have altered our understanding about Australia'a mid-Cainozoic (the Earth's current geological era representing 66 million years of the Earth's history) vertebrate diversity. A 15-million-year-old complete skull has provided new information about this highly distinctive group of mammals. No where else in the world is there such a rich, detailed and continuous fossil record of the changes in fauna, habitat and climate at a single locality.

There are large numbers of visible archaeological vestiges of Aboriginal occupation and sites of cultural significance at Riversleigh, particularly near the rivers. Aboriginal people currently live at the site, and appropriate involvement is sought in the management of identified cultural sites.

The Lawn Hill National Park is a 10 kilometre drive from Adels Grove and is the traditional land of the Waanyi Aboriginal people who called it Mumbaleeya Country (rainbow serpent country). This bush camp is the most remote camp you can find and it happens to be closely positioned beside paradise! This place is rich in botanical history and desolation. Adels Grove occupies an area of 80 acres and was originally gazetted in 1904 as a Miners Homestead Lease. In 1920 Albert de Lestang took the property as an experimental botanical garden. The name 'Adel' was created from his name. Albert planted many species of trees and shrubs and by 1939 he had over 1000 different species, some of which had come all the way from Africa. Canoeing and float tubes are available at 'The Beach' on Lawn Hill Creek. We asked if there were crocodiles at Lawn Hill Creek. The answer was; yes, the Johnston freshwater (freshies) crocodiles who are very timid near humans and not considered dangerous unless handled or cornered in some way and swimming in their waters is considered safe. Really? We didn't wait to find out!

Adels Grove is an eco-sensitive Tourist Camping Park on Lawn Hill Creek, located 10 kilometres downstream from the world heritage Riversleigh Fossil fields. We stayed in furnished river tents with proper beds.

When you get peckish, you can partake of a delicious chunky meat pie and maybe a sweet killer python lolly at the Cretaceous Café (another characterisation). The café had a range of basic food and drinks including pies, sandwiches, mujffins, coffee and cold drinks.

I'm not joking, the Australian Dunny Derby is a desired event. Teams take on the challenge of racing their decorated outhouses through a hilarious obstacle course to take home the title of the "Fastest Dunny". Every second September the Outback Festival blows into town, with outback activities from swag and brooms toss and wool bale rolling to live music and entertainment. Who said property boundaries had to be boring? The fence behind the Diamantina Heritage Truck and Machinery Museum is anything but. Designed by percussionist and composer Graeme Leak, the Musical Fence is a permanent wire fence that doubles as a musical instrument, free to the public to use and enjoy. This unusual musical installation is in fact a giant string instrument connecting fence wires to overhead acoustic resonators. It is very popular with tourists and welcomes a constant stream of visitors who can amuse themselves banging and bashing out tunes and crazy rhythms.

We travelled by coach from Winton to Longreach, a journey of two hours. We arrived at our final destination of Longreach, population of 2,960 people in the 2016 census, the town most famous for the Qantas Founders Museum, Outback Heritage Centre and of course the Australian Stockman's Hall of Fame. The town is named after the 'long reach' of the Thomson River on which it is situated. There is little to remind those living around Longreach today of the bulk of the region's human history. The landscape is in a weakened physical state with extraordinary powers of resilience, easily blemished and easily wiped clean. Longreach lies within the traditional tribal lands of the Iningai people. Iningai, (also known as Yiningay, Muttaburra, Tateburra, Yinangay and Yinangi), is an Australian Aboriginal language spoken by them. The Iningai language region covers landscape within the local government boundaries of the Longreach region, particularly the towns of Longreach, Barcaldine and Aramac, as well as the properties of Bowen Downs and catchments of Cornish Creek and Alice River. The Iningai people trod gently on this place for thousands of years, and were probably made up of small groups of clans and extended families who gathered occasionally for ceremonial events or trade. This marginal country, parched and devoid of interest, where the Iningai people walked over 50,000 square kilometres between the Great Dividing and the Forsythe Ranges, disturbing to the Iningai people for having been intruded by thousands of stock on to pristine waterholes and sacred sites, was left fragile with delicate tracings fainter than shadows. There's a vacant space in our history, and no one left with the knowledge of the Iningai sociology, history or customs. A handful of languages from the Mootaburra area, stone implements gathering dust on homestead verandahs, some deep scarred 'canoe' trees, scattered galleries and bora rings on the sandstone jump ups, and occasional native wells is all that is left.

Arrival was in the early evening when we were met by our guide and taken to our hotel. It's best to spend a week here because there is much to see. First it was the Australian Stockman's Hall of Fame built to honour the pioneering work of explorers, overlanders, settlers, Aborigines and the many who had made the area rich and prosperous. In 1974 Hugh Sawrey, a stockman and an artist, registered the name "Australian Stockman's Hall of Fame", and began encouraging people to contribute to the scheme, one of which was the famous stockman and businessman, R.R. Williams. R.M. Williams constructed a sandstone cottage having timber and black marble floors. It was replaced when, after a competition to design the building was won by Felko Bouman, construction of the Hall of Fame started in 1985. The building was opened by Queen Elizabeth 11 in 1988 and was so successful that, over the past thirty years, millions of people have visited the exhibition. It includes a model of Aboriginal cave paintings, the first fleet with computerized list of all the people on the first fleet), the early settlement in Sydney, the major explorations, the early pioneers, the pastoral expansion, and a focus on life in the outback up to the present day. Two hours is not long enough to see it all, and many will spend four or five hours wandering around the exhibition.

The Qantas Founders Museum is located across the road from the Stockman's Hall of Fame and has been operating since 1996. The first commercial flight by Queensland and Northern Territory Aerial Services Ltd (Q A N T A S), which started in Longreach took off from there on the 7th February 1921 and took 3 hours and 10 minutes to reach Winton.

The area's famous character (or infamous), was Captain Starlight, who became a bushranger along with Frank Pearson also know as Captain Starlight. Henry Arthur Redford, was a stockman and a drover and began his career as a cattle thief in 1870 in Queensland when he stole over 1000 cattle from Bowen Downs station where he was working as a stockman. He and two other men drove the cattle overland to South Australia. Readford was caught in 1872 and sent to trial but was found not guilty as, believe it or not, the jury were so impressed by he had achieved they let him go. Earlier the explorers Burke and Wills had died surmounting the exact same track.

In the 1892 novel Robbery Under Arms by Rolf Boldrewood, Readford was given everlasting fame. Boldrewood asserted that the Captain Starlight character in the book was a composition of several bushrangers, including Henry Readford, but that first in importance to inspire him was Thomas Smith, a bushranger known as Captain Midnight. The early chapters of the book were based on Readford's deeds, and the closing shoot out was based in the death of Midnight. An annual Harry Readford Cattle Drive keeps alive the memory of Readford's expoits as a drover. Starlight's Lookout said to used by Harry Readford during his cattle stealing exploits, is located 50 kilometres from Longreach. The lookout offers a splendid view of the surrounding countryside.

Dining out in the Welcome Home Café is more than meat pies and sausage rolls, with a menu for every Outback occasion – smoko, lunch, dinner and damper. Filled with old fashioned charm, friendly staff and tasty outback nosh, you can relax on one of Welcome Home's bentwood chairs or antique couches and enjoy a jacket potato decked out with veggies, chicken and sour cream., a Bushman's Burger, or Lamb Shanks for lunch. For dinner you'll be served up mouth-watering grills on 400-degree hot-stones at you table. I asked people in the town where the best restaurant is in Longreach, the answer was unanimously Harry's. There is a bar at the front and a linen tablecloth, date night atmosphere down the back. Their breakfasts are plentiful, but their evening meals are even stronger.

We held on as we jumped aboard the Cobb and Co Stagecoach for a ride through Longreach's bush scrub. It lets modern-day adventurers travel along the original Longreach – Windorah mail route in a restored stagecoach drawn by five stock horses. What a laugh! After the 45 minute dash, we had smoko of scones complete with jam and cream.

Thought your school was big? Consider this. The Longreach School of Distance Education is one of the largest classrooms in the world. Take a tour and be educated by going behind the scenes of the school that takes algebra lessons and spelling bees to the air, teaching children in remote locations across Queensland. Don't worry, surprise pop-up quizzes are not included.

Take a ten minute trip out of town to Camden Park Station, a working sheep and cattle station, where in 1970, the Queen visited; and so, it must be good right? The Duke of Edinburgh, the Prince of Wales and the Duchess of Cornwall have also ticked this spot off their Longreach bucket list. I suppose the Royals don't have bucket lists, or do they?

Bushranging forced a great influence in Australia, lasting for almost a century and prevailed in the eastern states. Bushrangers often attract public sympathy and are held in some esteem in some quarters due to the harshness and anti-Catholicism of the colonial authorities whom they embarrassed, and the romantic attitude of the lawlessness they represented. Some bushrangers, most notably Ned Kelly, expressed without reservation, that they represented themselves as political rebels. Attitudes to bushrangers show the conflicting attitudes of Australians regarding them. A number of bushrangers became folk heroes and symbols of dissent against the authorities admired for their bravery, courage and colourful personalities. However, in sharp contrast to romantic portrayals in popular culture, bushrangers tended to lead lives that were nasty, coarse and short, while some were notorious for their cruelty and bloodthirst. Attitudes in Australia toward bushrangers remain complex ambivalent.

We asked a local where's the best place to end the day in Longreach and he told us the Thomson River. We could have our pick of ships from the Longreach Explorer with Outback Aussie Tours or the Thomson Belle Paddlewheeler with Outback Pioneers to get us cruising down the Thomson. We saw many species of local birdlife as we sat back and relaxed and enjoyed the sunset. Definitely a photo opportunity. The best bits of Longreach are probably the sunsets, they are amazing. We were told to not to forget to visit the Longreach Powerhouse and History Museum for a dose of local history including the Heritage Listed Powerhouse, the original "town baths" and Nogo Cottage which is on the 32,000 hectare Nogo Station purchased by the Kinnon family in 2013. Alas our time ran out. A good excuse to visit again – it's easy to get there on the Spirit of the Outback.

Another way to spend our last day was to visit the CWA rooms. Located behind the Longreach Tourist Information Centre, the Country Women's Association, serves delicious scones and sponge cakes. Believe me you're in for a treat. There are restrooms there for your convenience, needless to say always clean and tidy. If you're lucky you might meet the Hat Lady of Longreach, Joyce Rogers who has 17 hats. Joyce who is well into her 80s, is a local athletics record holder, a CWA member for 56 years and is still involved in the daily running of the family sheep station, 100 kilometres west of Longreach. A lovely lady by all accounts.

Being a fan of murder mysteries, I began comparing the Spirit with the Orient Express. The film adaptation of Agatha Christie's Murder on the Orient Express would seemed to have confirmed once and for all that when it comes to iconic rail journeys, that particular trans-European trip reigns supreme. Or does it? At one's first look, the Orient Express would seem to have won. It's not just about murder, but a murder mystery – it just doesn't get more exciting than that. However, realistically, who wants to take a trip on a train with a body count? We are talking here about luxury travel in the golden age of rail – a stabbing seems more like the kind of thing you'd get in Pitt Street Sydney! When you're taking the train, excitement is the last thing you really want. Relaxation is what you want. Travelling on the Ghan is all about relaxing and taking your time; being murdered is the textbook definition of, running out of time. The other thing to note. You're meant to be able to solve the crime by following all the clues, then Murder on the Orient Express is widely acknowledged as being a story that doesn't really play fair. Let's just say this is the one time where Agatha Christie decided to keep the mystery going just a little too far. You might already know the answer, but if you don't know the answer, you might feel a little cheated. Looks like the Ghan is starting to win. There might be plenty of reasons to watch Murder on the Orient Express, but seeing the sights is definitely not one of them. The Ghan, on the other hand, travels through the heart of some of the most scenic landscapes in the world. Many Australian films have become international hits because they are set in the outback – it's an astonishing sight and there's no better way to see it than on the Ghan. In addition, there's the wildlife: wild camels, kangaroos, endless bush and a colourful collection of birds. The Ghan wins hands down. Whoever said getting there is half the fun probably wasn't talking about taking the train. There's something about the slow movement and sound of the rocking train. But Murder on the Orient Express has nothing to do with that. Most people would not quite realise that the story takes place on a train. And how can you compare train journeys not knowing even that you're on a train?

We boarded the train in Longreach on our journey to Rockhampton, 14 hours, 57 minutes. We travelled through historic towns to Barcaldine and stopped off here for a few days sightseeing – and there's plenty to see. We stayed at the Ironbark Motel, which is part restaurant, part bar, part tavern packed full of that home away from home feeling. They serve a great seafood basket, battered Barra, steak and pizza, washed down with a selection from the modest beer and wine list. Perfect! For morning tea we made tracks to the Barcaldine Bakery where the queue for coffee is often out the door – a good sign of what to expect in the cappuccino stakes. With their own 'Barcaldine Blend' pouring from the coffee machines, it's one of the best spots to get your day started if you're a coffee lover. They serve a superb English Breakfast tea too.

The town was named by an early settler Donald Charles Cameron who, having overlanded sheep from New South Wales, took up land in the district and named his property after Barcaldine in Argyllshire, Scotland. Prior to the arrival of Europeans, the area was home to the Iningai Aboriginal people. It was estimated that over 700 were living in the area at the time.

The Australian Workers' Heritage Centre, created to complement the Longreach Stockman's Hall of Fame, was opened in 1991. This interesting and award-winning museum celebrates the lives and proud heritage of ordinary working people – telling the stories of the railway workers and blacksmiths, the farmers, nurses and teachers who shaped the nation. Artefacts, artworks and multimedia presentations help to tell the story with displays including the shearers' strike of 1891, the history of postal workers, the role of women in war and Australia's working history, and the importance of Aboriginal stockmen.

The Heritage-Listed 'Tree of Knowledge', a ten metre tall ghost gum was poisoned by persons unknown. It had been a meeting place for shearers during the strike of 1891 and deemed to be of such significance to Australian industrial and labour history that an architect-designed Tree of Knowledge memorial was constructed using the original site in Oak Street and using the dead trunk of the original tree. The shearers' strike of 1891 was triggered at Logan Downs Station, near Clermont, when they were told they had to sign the Pastoralists' "contract of free labour" before commencing work – a move intended to reduce the influence of the unions in the sheds. It was a crucial event in the formation of the Australian Labor Party. The pastoralists imported non-union strike-breakers, who were protected by the police and troopers. There was retaliation in the form of crops and wool sheds being set alight. The colonial secretary then ordered the arrest of the union leaders who were charged with conspiracy and sedition and gaoled for three years, fined £200, and issued with twelve-month good behaviour bonds upon release. The failure of militancy to achieve the desired outcome prompted the labour movement to turn its attention to the pursuit of political power as a means of advancing the interests of working people. The sculpture, standing outside the town's railway station, features a striking 18 metre high cube in which 4000 suspended timbers of varying length from the tree canopy.

The six historic and interesting buildings in Barcaldine are all worth viewing – the Barcaldine Shire Hall, the Barcaldine and District Folk Museum, the Barcaldine Masonic Lodge, the Barcaldine War Memorial Clock unveiled in 1924 as a monument to the fallen of World War 1, and St. Peter's Anglican Church. The church is an excellent example of the use of timber in outback Queensland. The church was built in 1899 to a design by Edwin Hockings and its elaborate tongue-and-groove boards (three layers of solid European oak), and its craftsmanship make it a worthy example of Queensland's distinctive timber architecture. A rectangular building with a baptistery at the western end and flanked by small porches, it has a steeply pitched gable rood clad with corrugated iron which extends to cover the vestry on the southern side. There is a bell tower at the south east corner between the vestry and sanctuary.

Another interesting attraction is the Barcaldine Solar Farm, 5 kilometres east of Barcaldine on the Capricorn Highway. It has 79,000 solar modules which generate around 53,500 megawatts of clean, renewable power. The solar modules are designed to tilt in the direction of the sun, of which Barcaldine enjoys all round the year, thereby maximizing the energy.

We Passed Jericho, Alpha, and Emerald. Emerald is a prosperous, thriving service centre with a rural training college, a large number of farm machinery sales outlets, a huge irrigation dam and an airport. Established in 1879 as a base for the railway line, it grew to be the major regional centre of the Central Highlands and the gateway to the Central Western district. The Capricorn hinterland contains the largest sapphire gemfields in the world. Emerald grew very quickly in the 1980s and 1990s as a dormitory town for major new coal mines in the Bowen Basin. When land was taken up in the area around 1860, a settler named P. F. MacDonald, impressed by the greenness of the pastures, called his property Emerald Downs. The town takes its name from his property.

The traditional owners include the Gayiri people who occupied the area for tens of thousands of years before European colonization began in the nineteenth century. The first European to explore the area was Ludwig Leichhardt between 1843 and 1845. The British Colony of Queensland was established in 1859.

Finally Mt. Isa came into view. After a total of 8 hours and 40 minutes sitting in a bus from Longreach; our posteriors were worst for wear. Comfortable however. Population of over 18,000, Mt. Isa is known as the 'oasis of the outback', because it is situated in Queensland's immense North West in arid and romantic Outback Australia. Mt. Isa – often referred to by the locals as "The Isa", is located in the Gulf Country in north western Queensland and north eastern Northern Territory bordering the Gulf of Carpentaria. It is the largest township in western Queensland, and is a mining town with an air of self-esteem and resonance. It came aboutbecause of the vast mineral deposits found in the area. Mount Isa Mines is one of the most productive single mines in the world history, based on combined production of lead, silver, copper and zinc. Snuggled among the ochre-orange Selwyn Ranges, on the banks of the Leichhardt River, Mt. Isa is an area of energy, activity and blended nationalities and ideas. Although situated in an arid area, the artificial Lake Moondarra, 19 kilometres north of the city on the Lleichhardt River, provides both drinking water and an area for watersports, birdwatching and recreation.

Mining is the town's reason for being, and though it dominates the skyline and the local economy, Mt. Isa does not feel like just another outback mining town. It is a centre with excellent accommodation, good restaurants, and enough activities to keep even the most eager visitor busy for a week. 1925 kilometres north-west of Brisbane, Mt. Isa, presents innumerable difficulties for present day explorers, but the rewards can be exhilarating. It is listed by the Guinness Book of Records as truly extraordinary: it is still possible to go on an underground mining tour; to visit an underground hospital created during World War 11; to see what mining/company town the world's biggest city; LANDWISE. The debate is, that the city extends for 43,188 square kilometres, and that the road from Mt. Isa to Camooweal, a distance of 189 kilometres, is the longest city road in the world. Growing from strength to strength, the harsh but colourful landscape has attracted visitors each year. Although situated in an arid area, the artificial Lake Moondarra 19 kilometres north of the city on the Leichhardt River provides both drinking water and an aria for watersports, birdwatching and recreation.

The Mount Isa Regional Art Gallery features a magnificent display of artworks from local and regional artists. The gallery has something for everyone; sculptures, paintings, portraits, landscapes, abstract and Indigenous paintings. We enjoyed our visit to Mt. Isa, and when we left, we felt we had learnt very much more about the city.

The Beth Anderson Museum, which forms part of the Underground Hospital exhibit, features a fascinating range of antique medical equipment, including anatomy posters and a areal human skeleton, used to educate students. When we visited, we were taken into the Tent House, part of a community established in 1930 to accommodate the flourishing population. Hundreds of tent houses appeared, thanks to the ready availability of canvas which formed the walls and roof around a timber frame. A visit to the tourist centre which was phenomenal, has friendly staff who were very passionate about sharing everything within the centre and the region. The staff of the 5 star Outback Café, which served outstanding food, went out of their way please. We watched a small fozel (how they discovered old and ancient animals) demonstration.

The land around the city was home to the Kalkadoon Aboriginal tribe, who led a subsistence lifestyle on this land that white settlers considered was nothing but poor grazing land, with odd mineral deposit. As settlers moved further into their lands, the Kalkadoon tribe members set out with one of Australia's most successful armed forces to fight for their lands. In 1884, the tribe attacked a fortified position at Battle Mountain, and suffered terrible losses. The tribe's poor grazing land was exposed to diseases and disaster, and much of it was lost to the settlers. Times became hard for the settlers in the area over the following decades.

In 1923 prospector, John Campbell Miles, during an expedition into the Northern Territory, fell upon one of the world's richest deposits of copper, silver and zinc. Mt. Isa is in the top two of the largest copper mining and smelting operations in Australia. The mine is the main feature in the area, with the "stack" from the lead smelter (built in 1978), standing 270 metres tall, and is visible from up to 40 kilometres out of the city - amazing! Seeing is believing.

The beginning was tough for Mt. Isa, "no trains, no electricity, no water , no sanitation, other than a few miners' camps," said local historian Barry Merrick. Mt. Isa attracted immigrants from around the world, and at one stage it was the most multicultural city in Australia. "Lots of Finns, a lot of Europeans, Italians" said Barry Merrick, "even I think an Eskimo" he went on to say. Despite the fact that Mt. Isa is situated in an arid area, the City's Lake Moondarra, 19 kilometres to the north, provides both drinking water and a haven for water sports, bird watching and recreation.

Mt. Isa has the title of Rodeo Capital of Australia, the largest annual rodeo event in the Southern Hemisphere held in August. The Rodeo is where the love affair of the Australian Outback meets the courage and spirit of a mining town – east meets west and man meets beast. Competitors compete in the famous open-air, red dirt arena over four days of around the clock rodeo action. It is an event definitely worth seeing and a good reason to escape the cold down south and venture, then west to The Isa. We were not disappointed in the colour and extent of the competitive events and the sights and sounds of one of the most significant events for the bush. People from far and wide and many locals attend this great event. A well run event for meeting friendly people from here and around the world, thoroughly enjoyable, plenty of delicious food stalls selling the ubiquitous fairy floss and souvenirs and side show alleys. Each day riders go through heats culminating on the final day, when winners are presented and driven around the arena. It's a place to spend at least one full day and eve-ning, when you can sit back and relax and chat with a local. One for the bucket list. We are city ladies for most of our lives, however, we are now outback country lovers.

The Mt. Isa show is one of Mt. Isa's premiere events attracting over 6000 people every year, and is growing. In 1970 Queen Elizabeth and Prince Philip visited Mr. Isa. A few minutes after arriving at the airport, the Queen walked to the terminal fence to talk to part of the crowd gathered to meet her. The Queen visited, among other places, the Royal Flying Doctor Service operations section and tele-printer room where she met Winifred Seaton, who report-edly stunned at having spoken to the Queen. "I think we have all been kind of brainwashed that the Queen sits on a pedestal high up there above the heads of all ordinary people. She is just like anyone else. I was amazed at the casual way she walked through the base and spoke to us. She was mar-velous," Winifred said at the time. In the library is a photo-graph of Queen Elizabeth wearing a hard hat while on a tour of Mt. Isa mines during her royal visit to the city.

At Mt Isa we boarded the Inlander train which left at 12.40pm on a Saturday on the 21 hour, 977 kilometre journey to Townsville – a long way. However, the Inlander offered comfortable reclining seats in an open saloon car with overhead luggage rack, individual reading lights, pan-oramic windows, with toilets and washbasins and showers at the end of the carriage. For the adventurous, the Inlander provides an unparalleled way to explore the outback inland of Far North Queensland. It crosses the ranges and heads east to Townsville, as landscapes disappear over the horizon. Whether you're stopping off along the way or completing the journey, the train is airconditioned and comfortable. It's great to arrive feeling relaxed and refreshed. The Inlander service has boosted tourism and improved transport connections for travellers. Delicious hot meals are served for breakfast, lunch and dinner. Takeaway style meals and those snacks, fresh sandwiches, cheese and crackers, sliced buttered bread (naughty ones like cookies, biscuits and fruit cake), are avail-able all day from the Club Car to take back to your seat or eat in the Club Car, where you can meet other passengers and enjoy the social atmosphere.

We passed Duchess, a small rural town with a population of 23. Duchess (previously named Mairindi), was the name or nickname of the Aboriginal consort of pastoralist St John de Satge (who was nicknamed "The Duke"), who had run away an sought refuge at Kennedy's Calton Downs station.

Cloncurry was next. Known as the "Curry", it is 120 kilometres east of Mount Isa. Cloncurry is one of the few places that can claim to be as influential in shaping Australia. It is the birthplace of the Royal Flying Doctor Service and destination of the first Qantas flight. Cloncurry is a community that celebrates outback life, the true Australian way. You should spend a couple of days in Cloncurry to see the attractions of the town. I suggest you visit the Cloncurry Unearthed Visitor Information Centre and Museum where staff will advise you on things to see and do in the "Curry". A visit to the John Flynn Place Museum and Art Gallery, which pays tribute to the Reverend John Flynn and his team for their dedication and success in overcoming isolation and bringing communication, education and a health service to remote Australia, is a must. You must take a trip out to Chinaman Creek Dam, Cloncurry Lookout and Mary Kathleen Mine.

Julia Creek, is the next town we passed. At the latest census it had a population of 511 and its main industry is farming, especially beef and wool. The town is an important centre for cattle sales and stock trucking. Julia Creek was named after the niece of Donald McIntyre, the younger brother of Duncan McIntyre, the first white settler in the area. McIntyre took up a property called Dalgonally about 70 kilometres north of the present site of the town in 1864, only a few years after the ill-fated Burke and Wills expedition passed through the area.

Luckily our itinerary allowed us to stop off at Hughenden to see Hughie, the 7 metre Muttaburrasaurus and see an awe-inspiring fossil collection at the Flinders

Discovery Centre. Muttabuttasaurus Langdoni, was named after Doug Langdon who discovered the dinosaur who lived around 100 million years ago (give or take a million? I'm at a loss as to how this is calculated), during the Cretaceous period. Several specimens of this dinosaur have been found in central and northern Queensland, and a few teeth have been found in New South Wales. Muttaburrasaurus probably ate plants such as ferns, cycads and conifers. With prehistoric history over 100 million years old (here we go again), Hughenden and the Flinders Shire are located on the edge of a vast prehistoric inland sea, and was once home to many terrestrial dinosaurs as well as marine reptiles, making this country well known "Dinosaur Country".

That's not all there is to see in Hughenden; it is strategically placed to visit major attractions in the North West such as the Coolibah tree and the impressive sculptural piece, the Wirilla Comet Windmill Federation Rotunda. It is one of five sculptures and was erected to celebrate the Centenary of Federation in 2001. Designed and made by local artists Terry Lindsay and Sam Brown this splendid sculpture features two 20 foot blade windmills making a very impressive rotunda to walk through and rest under. In the Discovery Centre you can watch the famous Porcupine Gorge Light and Sound Show, which takes you back 500 million years (no comment) to the formation of what is known as "Australia's Little Grand Canyon".

We picked up the train again and travelled on through Torrens Creek, Pentland and Charters Towers. About two years ago I boarded a coach in Townsville, on a one hour, 55 minute ride to Charters Towers. There is lots to see in Charters Towers which is situated in northern Queensland, 134 kilometres from Townsville. There is ample hotel and motel accommodation which is comfortable, with break-fast room service, and some have restaurants and barbeque areas. The town was founded in the 1870s when gold was discovered by chance at Towers Hill on Christmas Eve 1871 by 12-year-old Aboriginal boy, Jupiter Mosman. The boom years were between 1872 and 1899. The production decline was similar across Australian gold mines, with rising costs and a fixed gold price eroding profitability. The town entered a long period of relative growth and little further development has occurred since. Known to the locals as The Towers, you won't find a huge backlit Charters Towers sign at the top of Towers Hill, but you will find one that says 'The World', as it was said that anything one might desire could be had in the 'Towers', leaving no reason to travel elsewhere. In 2016 the population was 8,120 people. With its summit 420 metres above sea level, this hard and unyielding peak is the very best way to get a lay of the land and catch a orange red sunset every evening. After sunset the town fires up, with daily screening of Ghosts After Dark, a film that covers the basics of Charter's gold boom. It's an appropriate location to hear about the gold rush as Towers Hill was the very spot the young Aboriginal boy named Jupiter (who the famous casino is named after) first discovered a chunk of alluvial gold back in 1871 and founded the town. Today, gold fossickers still arrive in significant numbers, equipped with metal detectors, in search of those golden nuggets – El Dorado.

Fitting for all ages, Whitbreads cordials are the perfect, refreshing beverage to take the edge off the outback heat, and yearn for the return of the past. That past is a vital part of Charters Tower's history, because Whitbreads has been serving fizzy drinks to the locals since 1896 to this day. All 25 flavours are manufactured, bottled and distributed from an independently-run factory in Charters. Their Splash Cola and Sarsaparilla flavours are made using a top secret formula, and have stayed almost exactly the same since the company was first established.

Charters Towers isn't just about gold, but gold is still a big part of the town's history. Back in the fossicking days, it was known as 'the vault' of Queensland, and there's nowhere better to appreciate this rich history than at the Venus Gold Battery. It's the closest you'll get to seeing exactly how gold was extracted out of Charters Towers. A tour will help you cherish in your mind a real appreciation for the effort that went into the operation and speaks to the mentality of prospectors at the time who would have done anything for a lump of gold.

Things are built bigger in the west, and Texas Longhorn Tours at Leahton Park is no exception. Run by Michael Bethel, the 110,000-acre cattle station sits 10 kilometres outside of Charters Towers. I took one of Leahton Park's outback safaris where you meet the largest herd of purebred Texas Longhorns in Australia. A steer called J.R. holds pride of place as having the longest horn in the world. Naturally, in the Outback, there's a good number of local ghost stories rustling around. You can hear some of the lore from locals at the pub, or join the Charters Towers Ghost Tour on Gill Street for a ghostly walk through the old city centre after dark. From ghosts who haunt their places of work, to a double murder in the Royal Private Hotel, to a bloodstained table that marks the spot of a cold-blooded shooting inside The World Theatre, there's no shortage of stories.

At Townsville, instead of flying home to Sydney, we decided to train it back. We boarded the Tilt train taking us to Brisbane, and then the XPT to Sydney, in preparation for our next rail escape. The Tilt Train is one of Australia's newest trains, the Tilt Train came into service between Brisbane and Rockhampton in 1997. The Tilt Train is administered by Queensland Rail and passengers enjoy comfortable reclinable seating, personal entertainment systems, galley service dining options and at-seat trolley service providing light snacks and refreshments. The Rockhampton and Bundaberg Tilt Train service offers passengers a choice of business or economy seating. The business seats are configured in a 2 x 1 arrangement and offer ample legroom, business seat customers also receive a complimentary juice and choice of newspaper or magazine on board. Reclinable economy seats on the Rockhampton and Bundaberg service are arranged in a 2 x 2 configuration and feature audio entertainment options. All seats face the direction of travel and feature a fold-down table and foot rest. The stainless steel-bodied trains have brought many new innovations to passenger travel in Australia. They are spacious and air-conditioned with video screens at each seat with individual audio control panels which offer passengers a range of entertainment.

CHAPTER 9

The Spirit of Queensland

I have been lucky to have travelled on some of the world's marvellous trains. I've experienced the excitement of rail on the Venice Simplon Orient Express, the Royal Scotsman, and at an alarming rate, sped through the Japanese countryside on a bullet train (320 kilometres an hour – although the newest bullet train, the SC Maglev reaches speeds of up to 603khs!). Here in Australia I've gone north to south on the Ghan and east to west on the Indian Pacific, and was able to experience The Sunlander train before she became an Australian memory. But I've never travelled on a train like this anywhere else in the world.

The first of her kind in the Southern Hemisphere, with regular services each week, the Spirit of Queensland was brought to replace The Sunlander, cutting the Brisbane to Cairns route down from 31 hours to a 25 hour journey. It's a great way to travel to visit friends and family or stop along the way to experience some of Queensland's impressive destinations including the Whitsundays, Townsville, Cairns or south to Bundaberg, Fraser Coast, Sunshine Coast and Brisbane with connections to travel further to the Gold Coast. Whether you're travelling to see the lights of the city of Brisbane, the Spirit of Queensland is an effortless and viable way to travel between Brisbane and Cairns. The speedier trip wasn't the only change between the two. Whereas The Sunlander has private sleeping compartments, the Spirit of Queensland has two classes and both remind me of something you'd usually see in the sky. The premium economy carriages feature leather seats, entertainment system with on demand movies, TV and music in the back of the seat in front of you, and a 30 degree seat recline. Meanwhile the Railbeds are reminiscent of business class seats on an airline, possible first class. Travel through ever-changing scenery with its strong features of rich golden soil and blue summer skies. The first class single berth cabin features all the mod cons. Of course, choose delicious meals from the Club Car menu on your journey from Brisbane to Cairns.

Long time dear friend Judy, accompanied me on this trip. We left Brisbane at 3.45pm and after passing the towns of the Queensland Sunshine Coast – Caboolture and Nambour, stopping at Cooroy for about half an hour, we passed Gympie. Seeing Caboolture from the train, it looked like an attractive classic village. Before European settlement the area was home to the Gubi Gubi Aboriginal language group. The first Europeans arrived in the early 1860s and were mostly timber cutters. I have visited the Sunshine Coast and its pristine beaches, scenic drives and unspoiled national parks on a few occasions. At Noosa, the Eumundi markets has more than 500 stalls selling artwork, craft, fashions by local designers and gifts – a shopper's paradise. Noosa's best known restaurant, Peter Kuruvita's the Noosa Beach House

Restaurant and Bar, offers breakfast and dinners in an elegant setting. It's on the point of the southern end of the Sunshine Coast that Caloundra dwells. With grassy stretches, sandy beaches, and surf spots aplenty, it's no wonder that Caloundra has become a all time favourite for Queensland families in particular Although with plenty of activities for all ages, the adventuresome will find no better place to holiday. Nambour is snuggled in the foothills of the Blackall Range and is a town with a whole lot of charm. Nambour was once known for its sugar mill, with purpose-built tram tracks transporting the sweet product through the town's centre. Today the historic tracks are being restored to their former glory paying homage to the region's past, but there's plenty of other reasons to add Nambour to your Sunshine Coast bucket list. The town is known for its artistic flair and talented creatives. Here you can follow the street art trail, or stop into one of the many nostalgic, vintage fashion or record stores in town.

We passed Howard on the way to Bundaberg. Friends Karyn, Margaret and "The Boyfriend", (long story), have been living there for quite some time. They telephoned us as we were going through on the train and we caught up on the latest. Howard is definitely one for my bucket list. Howard is located 281 kilometres north of Brisbane via the Bruce Highway and 28 kilometres west of Hervey Bay and its location is pretty accessible to those who are staying on the coast. The Hervey Bay area, has many small towns that run along the eastern coastline and aren't too far from Howard. In general, its location is pretty accessible to those who are staying on the coast. A charming historical town, it started life as a coal mining town, the last mine in the area closed in 1997, but today it is a service centre surrounded by sugar plantations and citrus orchards. Howard was named after William Howard who arrived in Maryborough in 1857, explored the local countryside and is credited with discovering the

Howard coal field in 1876. The area was originally inhabited by the Gubbi Gubbi people. Their traditional lands include Redcliffe, Bribie Island, Sunshine Coast, Noosa, Maryborough, Gympie, Caboolture and Petrie. 'Gubbi' means 'no' in the Gubbi Gubbi language, and 'Dyngungoo' means 'territory' in the Gubbi Gubbi language. Hence Gubbi Gubbi territory. Their culture protects the natural environment including their flora and fauna. The town's major tourist attraction is the delightful colonial home 'Brooklyn' which was once the home of Dame Annabel Rankin who was became a senator for Queensland from 1946 – 1971. Located next door to Brooklyn House, the original St Matthews, the only Anglican church in the district, built in 1883 on land donated by William Rankin.

Continuing on past Gympie North, Maryborough West and Bundaberg, where we would spend a few days. Our friend Rita, a long time resident of Bundaberg, came to meet us at the station. She dropped us off at our accommodation at the Grand Mercure C Bargara Resort, where we checked in and deposited our luggage in our rooms. The Resort is situated five minutes walk from Bargara (don't say the word too quickly!) Beach and Kelly's Beach. Highlights at this beachfront property include an outdoor swimming pool, in-room kitchens (who wants to cook when you're on holidays, nevertheless it was there for your convenience- that convenience I left at home!), private spa tubs and all mod cons. Rita took us back to her place and after chatting and catching up with news, she treated us to a sumptuous dinner before taking us back to the Resort. Bundaberg, population 70,921, a river city just minutes from the coast, is a typical, lively, country township with modern city elements. The Bundaberg Region has a civil association with Aboriginal culture and the heritage aspects of many local groups are mirrored in the names of local streets and communities. The Taribelang people comprised the main Aboriginal tribe in Bundaberg also having reported affiliations with neighbouring tribes Kabi-Kabi, Batjala and Waka-Waka. The name was formulated from a mixture of Aboriginal (bunda) and (berg/burg) either Anglo Saxon or German origin. The name was given to the town by John Charlton Thompson, the surveyor who laid out Bundaberg in the 1860s, and was applauded for his use of an Indigenous name. The first non-Indigenous man to visit the area was James Davis in the 1830s. He was an escaped convict from the Moreton Bay Penal Settlement who lived with the Kabi people to the south of the region. European settlement had a serious and devastating effect on the Indigenous people. Their deprivation of the land, exposure to new diseases and involvement in violent conflict, resulted in the death of a vast number of the Aboriginal people.

Gladys Moncrieff, said by Dame Joan Sutherland to be the Queen of Musical Comedy, was born in Bundaberg on 13th April 1892, and had her professional debut as a child singer in Dan Barry's touring production of East Lynne at the Queen's Theatre (a plaque has been placed on the building, now the Queens Theatre Arcade at 31 Woongarra Street). Our 'Glad', as she became known in Australia, at 19 years of age auditioned for JC Williamsons and was given a 3 year contract with Dame Nellie Melba's approval. At 22, she made her first recordings in London then returned to Australia to tour regularly with Williamsons and had an outstanding career in musical theatre and light opera. One of her final performances was at the opening of the Sydney Opera House in 1973. The Moncrieff Theatre was built in honour of Bundaberg's first lady of yesteryear, singer Gladys Moncrieff. The name Moncrieff Theatre was always a little unclear with regard to the true nature of the business. When the venue's façade was updated in October 2011, it seemed the perfect opportunity to undertake a name change. The

Moncrieff Entertainment Centre better describes the venue, as all forms of entertainment, including cinema (the first movie was Star Trek IV – The Voyage Home), live theatre, concerts and conferencing are held there. There's even been a wedding on stage at the Moncrieff!

The next day, friends Gae (Rita's cousin) and George took us sightseeing around Bundaberg. Among other places, we visited the award-winning Bundaberg Rum Distillery which I would recommend to prospective travellers to Queensland. We asked a local, what are the iconic things to do in Bundaberg, and she told us three things; the Bundaberg Rum Distillery, Bundaberg Brewed Drinks and the Hinkler Hall of Aviation. The guides at the distillery were attentive and friendly as they explained the process of making rum (no, we didn't get a taste). Next up was the Hinkler Hall of Aviation. Herbert John Louis (Bert) Hinkler AFC DSM was born in Bundaberg on 8th December 1892, the son of a sugar mill worker. By the age of 19 Bert had hand-built man-carrying gliders and already flew them successfully at picturesque Mon Repos Beach near Bundaberg. He was the first to fly solo from England to Australia, and the first person to fly solo across the Southern Atlantic Ocean. He died on the 2nd January 1933, after crashing into remote countryside near Florence Italy during a solo flight record attempt. The Hinkler Hall of Aviation has on display a small wooden piece of an early Hinkler glider that was carried on board the Space Shuttle Challenger and recovered after its breakup in 1986. Wander along Burnett River and lose yourself in the luxuriant botanical gardens or meander through the local shops and cafes in the architecturally attractive main street.

To satisfy my curiosity associated with the railways and tramways, what a better place to do it in than the Bundaberg Railway Museum. The Museum is Bundaberg City's first railway station, built in 1881, that houses a wide variety of railway items past and present. There are a few types of carriages, the Guard's carriage, originally a sleeper car, contains memorabilia, including uniforms going back to a coat with buttons pressed with the King's crown. In the signal box, there are phones, and morse code devices, a small wood fired cast iron heater used for the colder months and a jack that also screws sideways, used for minor derailments so that once it has lifted the wheels of a train, it can shift it back over to the rail. Dinnerware sets, some with the King's crown on them, others with the Queen's crown, locomotive number plates and many other railway memorabilia, including tools of various types; locomotive spanners, heavy jacks and track work tools, interlocked signal cabin recovered from Lowmead Station, are on display. The last Centralized Traffic Control panel used for railway signalling, and modern day transponders are also on view. A 1921 guard's van, originally a sleeping car, and a butter car insulated with cow's hair which stays cool even without the ice blocks are on show. Static displays outside include a diamond crossing for cane trams to cross the Government lines and various couplings, buffers, drawhooks and air hoses used on older rolling stock. There are books including office records, engine driver's manuals, timetables and rule books. You can travel back in time and take a ride on the fully restored Purrey Steam Tram, considered to be the only operational one of its kind in the world. Morning tea is served in this marvelous historic setting as you listen to the sounds of hissing steam, the blast of the whistle and the clickerty clack of the tram on the tracks. This is where I found out what a hobo stick was. It was because of the problems of homeless people wandering the country looking for jobs and would try hitching a ride in cargo carriage. The carriages were changed so a bolt at the top of the door would drop when the door was closed, allowing the door to be opened only a little way. At this point, I was expecting that the hobo stick was used to prod the homeless person away from the carriage, instead the stick was used to reach the bolt through the narrow opening to release the door to open the rest of the way. I was happy to have stopped at this hidden treasure in North Bundaberg, operated by a dedicated group of volunteers. All the buildings of the original station, built in The Museum is a sanctuary for train buffs.

We continued on to Rockhampton on the Tropic Of Capricorn, where we spent a couple of days. It's the unofficial Capital of Central Queensland and has a feast of glorious Victorian-era buildings. Some say (and one should not really enter into this debate) that Rockhampton is the most beautiful regional centre in Australia. The concentration of beautiful old buildings, the tree lined streets, all make this area of Rockhampton's CBD one of the pleasurers of any visit to the city. Rockhampton was named as a simple combination of "rock" (it was located where there was a rock barrier across the Fitzroy River) and the English suffix "Hampton" which denotes a place near water, to produce a name which means "place near the rock in the river".

The region of Rockhampton and Capricorn Coast is the traditional land of the tribes and clans of the Darumbal (or Dharumbal) Aboriginal people. The British colonisation of the area began in 1853, when the Archer brothers, Charles and William, who were seeking grazing lands arrived in the Rockhampton area. They were acting on information from earlier expeditions by Ludwig Leichhardt and Thomas Mitchell, who had explored the area in 1844 and 1846 and noted suitable land for grazing. Matthew Flinders, who circumnavigated and charted Australia, made contact with the Darumbal people in 1802. Observations by Matthew Flinders and subsequent explorers noted that their appearance and nature as distinctly different to the natives around Gladstone and Miriam Vale. European settlement was justifiably opposed by the Darumbal people who were often recorded by explorers and settlers as a violent warring tribe, and as recently as 1904 in the Early History of Rockhampton, JTS Bird described Indigenous tribes of Central Queensland as perpetrators of 'murder and outrage'. While these words came from years gone by, they nevertheless depict a landscape of European attitudes towards the Aborigines as being a subclass of human without the right to defend their lands from invasion. There was often conflict between the Aborigines and the settlers.

The Dreamtime Cultural Centre which is set in 12 hectares of gardens, including a small waterfall and a pond, introduces the visitors to the culture of Central Queensland Aborigines and the people of the Torres Strait Islands. We joined a tour where we were shown how to make and play a didgeridoo (I was breathless) and how the local Aborigines use the plants of the area and how they built their dwellings. The building was constructed to recreate a cave in the Carnarvon National Park which, according to Aboriginal legend, is haunted by an old Aborigine who only appears to women. He apparently lost his wife to a younger man and spends eternity seeking to find her once again.

With abundant grazing lands and waters from the Fitzroy River and its many tributaries and lagoons, the region continued to expand rapidly. In 1858, the town of Rockhampton was officially proclaimed. When gold was discovered in 1859, at Canoona, miners rushed to the new field. The Canoona field proved to be very disappointing and thousands of would-be aspiring gold seekers were left stranded in Rockhampton. Although many returned south, others stayed, adding to the new town's population. Conflict with Aboriginal people in the region continued and further massacres occurred. In 1859, John Arthur Macartney attempted to stock his cousin's Belmont property just to the north of Rockhampton when a shepherd was killed by local Aboriginal men. 2nd Lieutenant Frederick Carr of the Native police together with his troopers, the Macartneys, Peter Fitzallan MacDonald and Henry Brisdon, formed an armed group which set out to track down those responsible. One report of this incident describes how around a hundred of the tribe were rounded up and "it ended in the usual way and the bulk of the wild mob were shot" (Place Names, (2021, para. 13), states that...."it ended in the usual way..."). During the 1860s and 70s, Rockhampton developed as the main port for the developing Central Queensland hinterland, the main export at that time being wool. The Darumbal Dreamtime Centre in Rockhampton, built to commemorate and educate people about the rich culture that pre-existed the arrival of Europeans, is the largest Aboriginal cultural centre in Australia.

Rockhampton has a number of Heritage Buildings, one of them being the Royal Bank of Queensland, which was built in 1889 to capitalize on the riches from the gold mine at Mount Morgan. It is a typical Rockhampton building of the era with a neo-classical style and a colonial influence. Like most banks at the time the upper storey was the residence of the manager and the ground floor was for banking. Another building worth visiting is St Paul's Anglican Cathedral constructed out of sandstone and built between 1879-83 in classic Gothic stye. The church was one of the first large public buildings in Rockhampton to use locally-quarried sandstone from the Stanwell Quarry in its construction. Amusingly this building was a response by the congregation to the criticism that the previous, somewhat modest, church had been too small. St Josephs Catholic Cathedral, built in 1889-90 is also worth a visit. It has stood for over a century in Rockhampton and its architecture and beauty and the magnitude of its stature, make it a focal point of the Rockhampton Diocese. St. Joseph features a particularly fine black and white chequered Italian marble floor, sandstone block construction and authentic leadlight windows hand-crafted in England. Both these Cathedrals and their characters remind us of the transcendence of God.

Then we stopped at St Lawrence and continued on past McKay, Proserpine and Bowen. Bowen is a coastal town located in the Whitsunday Region, halfway between Townsville and Mackay. It was previously occupied by the Biri Aboriginal language speaking people. Next we stopped at Home Hill, then Ayr, Giru (stop), and finally arriving at Townsville.

The trip on the Spirit of Queensland was simply excellent, and a relaxed and smooth ride, the train is amazingly quiet on the tracks. I was very surprised by the amount of legroom in the carriage – very clean. The meals in the buffet car were airline style but quite tasty and well presented. It's a must try experience.

We decided to spend a week in Townsville, although, it was not long enough to see all the attractions of this tropical town – on the list for my next rail odyssey.

Townsville was originally inhabited by the Wulgurukaba, Bindal, Girrugubba, Warakamai and Nawagi peoples – difficult to pronounce words are not my forte! James Cook visited the Townsville region on his first voyage to Australia in 1770, but did not actually land here. In 1846, James Morrill was shipwrecked from the Peruvian, living in the Townsville area among the Bindal peole for 17 years before deciding to return to British society when the frontier of colonization came to the region. The city was named after a notorious slave trader, Robert Towns, who was well-known for the practice of 'blackbirding', which is Australian for abducting South Sea Islanders and forcing them to work on sugar cane plantations. Robert Towns imported the first boatload of South Sea Islanders into Townsville to labour on the cane and cotton farms. There were 56 Islanders who arrived on the Blue Bell which had brought them from the New Hebrides and Loyalty Islands. Charges were made against Henry Ross Lewin, the recruiter for Robert Towns, that some of the Islanders had been kidnapped to work on plantations, and some deaths were attributed to lack of proper nourishment – the Islanders received only cornmeal for food. Other evidence was given by employees of the plantation company who claimed the labourers were treated well and a verdict of death by natural causes was declared.

Townsville is approximately 350 kilometres from Cairns and lies on the shores of Cleveland Bay. It has several large valuable public assets including the James Cook University, the Great Barrier Reef Marine Park Authority and historic sightworthy buildings such as the Townsville Post Office built in 1886, the former Bank of New South Wales built in 1887 and the former Bank of Australasia built in 1905. The Museum of Tropical Queensland is a large tropical aquarium holding many of the Great Barrier Reef's native flora and fauna. It is built around a display of relics from the sunken British warship HMS Pandora, the most prominent landmark of the area and a popular place for exercise, The Townsville Sports Reserve.

One of the most impressive churches of Townsville is the Sacred Heart Roman Catholic Cathedral built in 1896-1902, along with the St. James' Anglican Cathedral built in two stages 1887-1892 and 1959-1960.

The Townsville Civic Theatre is North Queensland's premier cultural organization, and since its opening in 1978. The Theatre has been a centre of entertainment and performing arts, providing a facility to further develop the arts in Townsville and the North. The absorbingly named Full Throttle Theatre Company is a professional theatre company based in Townsville where they showcase the talents of local actors, designers, directors and playwrights. We were lucky enough to see one of the major shows which are presented four times a year.

We visited the Perc Tucker Regional Gallery first up. It is a public art gallery of Townsville and focuses on artwork pertinent to North Queensland and the Tropics. The region has many renowned festivals, many which celebrate the international heritage of many that call North Queensland home. The Annual Greek and Italian Festivals are popular with the locals and tourists alike. The city has many restaurants and a vibrant pub and night club scene, concentrated along Palmer Street, Flinders Street and the Strand. The Australian Festival of Chamber Music is an international chamber music festival held over ten days each July in the Townsville Entertainment Centre, has been running since 1991, attracts many acclaimed international and Australian musicians. There are plenty of sporting facilities in Townsville, a Rugby League Club, Townsville and District Rugby Union Club, Touch Football Club and three tennis clubs, a go cart track and motocross track.

Townsville has a significant World War 11 history. In July 1942, three small Japanese air raids were conducted against Townsville, which was by then the most important air base in Australia. On 25th July 1942, two Japanese Kawanishi Flying Boats dropped 15 bombs which landed near the mouth of the Ross River. On 28th July, a Japanese plane dropped eight 230-kilogram bombs near bushland outside the town. In 1896, Japan established its first Australian consulate in Townsville, primarily to serve some 4,000 Japanese workers who migrated to work in the sugar cane, turtle, and pearling industries. With the introduction of the White Australia policy, the demand for Japanese workers decreased, causing the Consulate to finally close in 1908. However, a Consular Office of Japan was established in Cairns in 1997 and is responsible for overseeing the relationships between Japan and North Queensland. It serves the interests of Japanese nationals living in North Queensland and offers assistance to Australians who seek to visit or learn more about Japan. During World War 11, the city was host to more than 50,000 American and Australian troops and air crew, and it became a major staging point for battles in the South West Pacific. A large United States Armed Forces contingent supported the war effort from seven airfields and other bases around the city and in the region.

On Christmas Eve 1971, Tropical Cyclone Althea, a category 4 cyclone, (category 5 being extremely dangerous and the strongest winds which are very destructive with typical gusts over open flat land of more than 280 kilometres per hour), a severe tropical cyclone with very destructive winds with typical gusts over open flat land of 225-279 kilometres per hour, caused significant roofing loss, structural damage, dangerous airborne debris and widespread power failures.

In 1973, Indigenous activists Eddie and Bonita Mabo established the Black Community School in Townsville, where children could learn their Indigenous culture rather than white culture. Eddie Koiko Mabo was born on the 29th June 1936 in the community of Las on the island of Mer in the Torres Strait (also known as Murray Island), and was raised by his Uncle, Benny Mabo, following the death of Eddie's mother during childbirth. At the age of 16, Eddie was exiled from Mer for breaking customary law. He moved to mainland Queensland, where he worked at various jobs, including deck hand, cane cutter and railway labourer. In 1959, aged twenty-three, Eddie married Bonita Nehow and they eventually settled in Townsville, where they raised ten children. Eddie Mabo worked as a gardener at James Cook University in the 1970s and 1980s, and it was at the university in 1974 that he first learned of the implications of the terra nullius doctrine (terra nullius is a Latin term meaning "land belonging to no one" - British colonization and subsequent Australian land laws were established on the claim that Australia was terra nullius, justifying acquisition by British occupation without treaty or payment), which held that he did not legally own the land he believed was his under the traditional land inheritance system of his people. Eddie became a spokesperson for the Torres Strait Islander community and was involved with the trade union movement and the Aboriginal and Torres Strait Islander Advancement League. He also helped to found the city's Aboriginal and Islander Health Service, and co-founded and directed the Townsville Black Community School. Imagine how you would feel if someone took something very important and valuable from you. What if they told everyone it didn't belong to you in the first place so they were allowed to take it? What if that same person was in a position of power over you so you were powerless to do anything about it? How do you think it would feel if, a long time later, the truth was finally revealed? How important is it that our country's values, laws and historical stories reflect the truth? In 1981 a land rights conference was held at James Cook University and Eddie Mabo made a speech to the audience where he explained the land inheritance system on Murray Island. As a consequence of this in terms of Australian common law doctrine, was taken note of by one of the attendees, a lawyer, who suggested there should be a test case to claim land rights through the court system, and Mabo decided to take on the Australian Government. Mabo and his companions claimed that the Meriam people had continuously inhabited and exclusively possessed these lands, lived in permanent settled communities and had their own political and social organization. On these grounds, the Mabo case sought recognition of the Meriam peoples' rights to this land. Perth-based solicitor Greg McIntyre was at the conference and agreed to take the case; he then recruited barristers Ron Castan and Bryan Keon-Cohen. The James Cook University Douglas campus library is now named after Mabo. In the 1971 Gove land rights case, Justice Blackburn ruled that Australia was terra nullius prior To European settlement. This judgement was unsuccessfully challenged by subsequent cases in 1977, 1979 and 1982. However, on the 20th May 1982, Eddie Koiki Mabo and four other Indigenous Meriam people began their legal claim for ownership of their traditional lands on the island of Mer in the Torres Strait. On the 3rd June 1992 the High Court of Australia ruled in favour of Eddie Mabo in Mabo v Queensland (NO 2) recognizing native title in Australia for the first time. Native Title recognizes that Indigenous Australians have a prior claim to land taken by the British Crown since 1770. It replaces the "legal fiction" of terra nullius, which formed the foundation of British claims to land ownership in Australia. The great significance of the Mabo case finally acknowledged the history of Indigenous dispossession in Australia, abolished the legal fiction of "terra nullius", and altered the foundation of Australian land law. The Mabo verdict was an important period that served as a dividing line for Australian law, politics and history. The subsequent apology by Prime Minister Kevin Rudd further reinforced the totality of facts as they are and what it meant for our story as Australians. Nevertheless while the understanding as a nation of the fact that the British did not arrive to vacant land, has not made much difference to the day to day reality of most Indigenous Australians.

Magnetic Island

Went over to Magnetic Island, 8 kilometres offshore from Townsville, by one of Sealink's high-speed catarmans – it was paradise in only 20 minutes! The original Indigenous inhabitants of Magnetic Island, were the Wulgurukaba people, who lived here for thousands of years before European settlement and named the island Yunbenun (Magnetic Island). The island had a transient population well before European exploration of the area. They had seasonal camps at a number of bays, and travelled between the island and mainland using canoes. The first European accounts of the island come from Captain James Cook who, in 1770, while navigating the Australian coast, called the island Magnetical Island, as a magnetic pull interfering with his vessel's compass appeared to emanate from the island.

The island is a nature lovers heaven, with secluded beaches, kilometres of bushland hikes and an abundance of wildlife. I stayed one night at Peppers Blue on Blue Resort, which is tastefully laid out at the water's edge overlooking the Coral Sea and private marina, where you can relax by the large lagoon style pool with a cocktail and book and de-stress at the resorts on-site day spa, which provides relaxing massages and invigorating facials. You can sup, ski and sail on this stress free laid back island with its mild climate and staggering white sand beaches and bays, and..........boutique resort wear shops – I like this place already!

Maggie, as the locals call it, is home to the largest colony of koalas in Northern Queensland and the Magnetic Island Koala Hospital who work tirelessly rehabilitating injured and abandoned koalas. Yes, you can get a photo with and cuddle a koala or take a walking tour along the forts walk and see them in the wild. You can get up close and personal with wallabies and wombats, and spot humpback whales as they migrate through the Winter.

Maggie has a diverse and pulsating community of artists, guided by the natural beauty and history of the island. There are a number of warm and friendly local galleries, where you can shop (just my style) and admire local art just metres from the beach. Magnetic Island is well known for its angling opportunities – fish around the island include; marlin, mackerel, coral trout, tuna and many more.

We boarded the train again and continued on to Ingham, approximately 110 kilometres north of Townsville. Prior to European settlement, the Ingham area was inhabited by the Warakamai people. The town was named after William Bairstow Ingham and is the administrative centre for the Shire of Hinchinbrook. Next we passed Cardwell along the coast to Tully, a town in the Cassowary Coast region 140 kilometres south of Cairns. The Tully River was named after Surveyor-General William Alcock Tully in the 1870s. Tully is one of the larger towns of the Cassowary Coast and the economic base of the region is agriculture: sugar and bananas are the prominent crops. Tully is perhaps best known fo being one of the wettest towns in Australia and home to the 7.9 metre tall Golden Gumboot.

And now to Cairns. We re-boarded the Spirit of Queensland in the morning, ready for the journey to Cairns. Stops along the way were Ingham, Cardwell, Tully, Babinda,

Gordonvale and finally Cairns in the late afternoon. A comfortable journey of 25 hours, 1681 kilometres. Cairns is a provincial city, with a linear urban layout that runs from the south at Edmonton to the north at Ellis Beach. The city is approximately 52 kilometres from north to south; it has experience a recent urban sprawl, with suburbs occupying land once used for sugar can farming. Cairns is on the east coast of Cape York on a coastal strip between the Coral Sea and the Great Dividing Range. The Mulgrave River and Barron River flow within the greater Cairns area but not through the Cairns CBD. The city's centre foreshore is located on a mud flat. This infusion of mud has been wonderful for the mangrove ecosystem, but not great for tourists who would rather see a sandy beach than muddy tidal swamp. The arguments purported by developers are that the mudflats are an artificial ecosystem that is not integral to the mangrove forest. But environmentalists insist that the area has been in its current form long enough to be home to thousands of species of mud-dwelling creatures, and to dump sand on top of them is unlawful premeditated killing of hundreds of species of animals. The Esplanade street as it is today, was the first to be surveyed in Cairns in October 1876. It was named Troughton Esplanade after the Travelling Superintendent of the Australian Steam Navigation Company, Captain Fred Troughton. The original city plans of the history of Tropical North Queensland were lost and the name Troughton was dropped, resulting in the simple name "Esplanade". Photos recovered by Cairns locals and The Cairns Post newspaper reveal that the esplanade was once a sandy beach, similar to Cairns Northern beaches such as Machans Beach. The area is known in the Yidiny language as Gimuy by the people who inhabited the region before colonisation are the Gimuy-Walubarra clan of the Yidinji people. The city was founded in 1876 and named after Sir William Wellington Cairns, the

Governor of Queensland from 1875 to 1877. It was formed to serve miners heading for the Hodgkinson River goldfield, but declined when an easier route was discovered from Port Douglas. At a later date it developed into a railhead and major port for exporting sugar cane, gold, minerals and agricultural products from surrounding coastal areas and the Atherton Tableland. From 1770 to the early 1870s the area was known to the British simply as Trinity Bay. The arrival of beche de mer fisherman – the illegal fishing of sea-cucumbers (beche-de-mer). Illegal fishing by Papua New Guinea skilled fishermen in the Torres Strait protected zone by the Department of Marine Biology, James Cook University of North Queensland, Townsville, from north to south. These reefs were extensively fished for dugongs, turtles and fish by the coastal villages of the Western Province.

During World War 11, the Allied Forces used Cairns as a staging base for operations in the Pacific, with United States Army Air Forces and Royal Australian Air Force operational bases (now the airport), as well as a major military seaplane base in Trinity Inlet, and United States Navy and Royal Australian Navy bases near the current wharf. Combat missions were flown our of Cairns in support of the Battle of the Coral Sea in 1942.

The population in June 2019 was 153,951 people. Aboriginal and Torres Strait Islander people made up 8.9% of the population. 67.9% of people were born in Australia. The next most common countries of birth were England 4.0%, New Zealand 3.1%, Papua New Guinea 1.5%, Phillipines 1.2% and Japan 1.1%. 76.9% of people only spoke English at home. Other languages spoken at home included Japanese 1.6%, Mandarin o.8%, Italian 0.7%, Korean 0.7% and German 0.6%. The most common responses for religion were No Religion 32.1%, Catholic 22.4% and Anglican 13.2%.

Cairns is a popular tourist destination because of its tropical climate and access to tropical rainforest and the Great Barrier Reef. We couldn't visit Queensland without visiting the Great Barrier Reef, not only is it a UNESCO World Heritge site, but unfortunately, it's an endangered one as well. We knew that this might have been a once-in-a-life-time activity, so I spent hours researching companies to try and guess which one would give me the best Great Barrier Reef tour, also taking into account all the different things to do at the Reef. I'd like to share the tour I ended up taking and my experience with it. We booked this tour through GetYourGuide. I like how they often offer free cancelation up until 24 hours beforehand and also share the name of the local tour operator. More than 2300 kilometres of jaw-dropping, living coral, hundreds of tropical islands with turquoise glittering shores and white crescents of sand, is The Great Barrier Reef. There's no doubt that The Reef is one of the seven natural wonders of the world. For a good reason this sits at the top of my bucket list. The Great Barrier Reef is the largest reef system on the planet, and parts of the reef could be up to half a million years old! It is a landmark so immense that it can be seen from outer space. There are over 3000 individual reefs in total and 900 tropical Great Barrier Reef islands including the breathtaking Lizard Island, picturesque Lady Elliot Island and Tropical Heron Island.

The Great Barrier Reef is situated in the Coral Sea off the coast and stretches all the way along the Queensland coast from Bundaberg in the south up beyond the northern tip of Australia, to near the south coast of Papua New Guinea. But what are coral reefs? Coral reefs are built by coral polyps as they secrete layers of calcium carbonate beneath their bodies. The corals that build reefs are known as "hard" or "reef build-ing" corals. The coral polyps survive by forming a symbiotic relationship with microscopic algae called zooxanthellae.

There are 411 types of hard coral, one-third of the world's soft corals, 134 species of sharks and rays, six of the world's seven species of threatened marine turtles, and more than 30 species of marine mammals live in the Great Barrier Reef. Astounding! Stingers (marine animals like irukandji and box jellyfish), can be present at any time during the year but are mostly seen from October to May. You are advised to wear protective clothing.

Port Douglas

I had never been to Port Douglas, and decided that it was time to do so. Port Douglas lies north of Cairns and is a little less touristy. The history of Port Douglas is a series of expansion and contraction. When gold was discovered on the Hodgkinson River in 1876, the rush was on to find a port for its dispatch. In 1877 Christie Palmerston carved the Bump Track down to the coast and Port Douglas was quickly settled by merchants. By 1882 there were 14 hotels in town and it was a boom period for Port Douglas, which overtook Cairns as the main port for gold and tin mining. But in 1885, the rail link from the Tablelands was joined to Cairns and development in Port Douglas soon declined. Tick fever ravaged the cattle herds and farmers turned to sugar cane, with the first crush at the Mossman Mill in 1897. A small rail line was built from the mill to the Port Douglas wharf in 1900 for sugar, freight and passengers, and the population of the Port grew to 331 with 4 pubs. The export of sugar had revived the Port. But during the massive cyclone of 1911, sixteen inches of rain fell in 24 hours, two people were killed and many houses were damaged, some never to be rebuilt. In 1920 the business centre moved to Mossman to be near the mill. In 1984 the new Cairns International Airport brought tourists from around the world to revive Port Douglas. Port Douglas is now a popular destination for Australian and International visitors keen to visit the Great Barrier Reef and the Daintree World Heritage Rainforest.

The Yirrganydji People

I first learnt about the Yirrganydji people on this tour who were the original inhabitants of the coastal strip of land between Cairns and Port Douglas, including Freshwater Creek and the Barron River. The Yirrganydji people had an intimate knowledge of their lands and waters, flora and fauna, seasons and weather. They were both a rainforest-dwelling and seafaring people, utilising the resources of both environments for their food, clothing and other needs.

In the wet summer season (Gurabana Bana – water) from November to April, they lived in semi-permanent shelters constructed from loya cane, palm fronds and paperbark. A hunter-gatherer society, the Yirranydji foraged up and down the coast, following seasonal food sources. The creeks, rivers, coast and sea yielded barramundi, bream, jewfish, grunter, catfish, cod, eels, turtles, prawns, crayfish, oysters and periwinkles. They hunted wallabies, bandicoots, scrub pythons, sand goannas, blue-tongued lizards, brush turkeys and various other birds. Towards the end of the dry winter season (Guraminya Minya – meat) from May to October, vegetation would be burnt off. This process would stimulate new growth, providing fresh pasture for the many animals on which the Yirrganydji depended.

The skyline is low-rise because local laws restrict buildings to palm tree height. Port Douglas is actually closer to the more unharmed Outer Great Barrier Reef. Tours from Port Douglas can give you a less crowded experience and bring you to areas of the Reef that are better preserved. We took a tour on the luxury catamaran, "Wavedancer", to the coral cay

Low Isles where we listened to a talk by a marine biologist. We discovered sea life at the water's edge on a guided beach walk and enjoyed a buffet lunch. Water, pastries, salty snacks and fruits were provided as well. Delicious I must say. The tour was six hours and gives you the longest stay on the Reef of all available tours. On this tour we visited two outer Reef locations, and aside from snorkeling, we were able to take a glass-bottom boat tour, feed some fish and prawns.

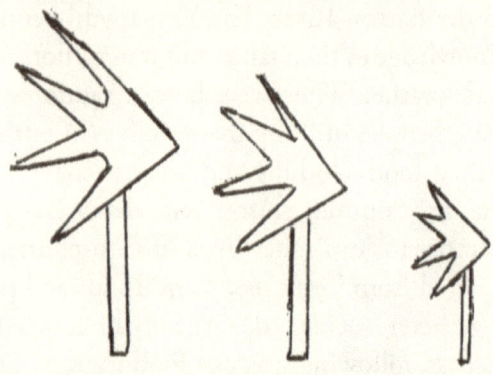

The outer reefs are characteristically more colourful and less damaged than the closer reefs, which naturally suffer from coral bleaching. Overall, the Outer Barrier Reef cruise was outstanding and there was time to relax on deck, and we had ample time to snorkel at both Reef sites and also plenty of time to enjoy lunch.

A visit to Cairns and Tropical North Queensland is not complete without a journey on the world famous historic Kuranda Scenic Railway especially when you choose to upgrade to some old fashioned first class Private Rail Carriages in Gold Class with sparkling wine and canapès in club style seating. On this 90-minute train journey you are in for a treat as you pass through some beautiful tropical scenery surrounded by majestic mountains with cascading waterfalls and perilously deep gorges. This day tour is an experience for everyone to enjoy, and as you sit in your comfortable seats you can listen to the story of how the railway tracks and tunnels were carved out of the rainforest and the granite mountains by hand to build the wonderful trip you get to still enjoy today. The best thing we did was to combine the rail trip with a Skyrail Gondola ride so you can see the magnificent rainforests just like the birds do from up above. Far North Queensland's World Heritage-Listed rainforest called the Wet Tropics, are amongst the oldest on earth and home to an incredible range of plants and animals. Twelve hundred species of flowering plants, eight hundred different rainforest trees, spectacular orchids, strangler figs, exotic palms and hundreds of unique creatures inhabit this lush verdant world. These natural wonders are so close that you can almost touch them. The tour includes a commentary which gives information on the history of the railway's construction, a trip map and a map of Kuranda. The village of Kuranda has a variety of attractions and unique shopping experiences (did someone say shopping!).

From Cairns, some years before, I went by cargo ship, the Trinity Bay, on a 40 hour trip up to Cape York and the Torres Strait Islands. This might seem a bit industrial, but don't be alarmed, this working ship was fully equipped with passenger cabins, a dining lounge and the best buffet, an outside deck and media room. You wouldn't believe but some trickster put on the Titanic video! It stopped along the way to deliver supplies to some remote communities, and on one occasion, a small truck was delivered to the small community of Lockhart River population of 724 people consisting mostly of Aboriginal and Torres Strait Islanders whose ancestors were forcibly moved to the area beginning in 1924. It was originally an Anglican Mission relocated from 'Old Site' south of Cape Direction, to its present location on Quintell

Beach. It was a very windy day and as the ship couldn't dock because the water was too shallow, the truck had to be lowered on to a barge. This operation was very tricky. The truck was lowered slowly on to the barge, while all the time the hoist was swinging from side to side. What precision! They say it's all about the journey, not the destination, but in this case, it's just as much about the destination. We sailed through the Torres Strait and disembarked on Horn Island and Thursday Island, where we learnt about pearl farming on Roko Island and getting that highly sought-after photo at the northernmost point on the Australian continent. I took a helicopter flight over Lockhart River and other islands in the area: Chapman Island, Lloyd Island, Rocky Island, Sherrard Island and Sunter Island. I would urge every Australian to visit Cape York and the Torres Strait.

CHAPTER 10

More Fabulous Queensland Trains

The Gulflander

On another visit to North Queensland I boarded the legendary Gulflander train, which was a journey like no other. One steps back into Queensland's pioneering history as it travels the Heritage-listed Normanton to Croydon line. Originally built to connect the once bustling river port of Normanton with the rich gold fields of Croydon, and affectionately said to go from 'nowhere to nowhere'. Today the Gulflander is a tourism icon. From wetlands and grasslands to the arid Savannah, the 1950 railmotor, also know as the 'Tin Hare', ventures through countryside that most people would never see. On this evocative rail journey, you step back in time and discover an area steeped in pioneering history and heritage. The Heritage-listed Normanton Railway Station is a bonanza of history and architecture. The Normanton Officer-in-Charge, Station Master and driver of the Gulflander, Ken Fairbairn, takes you on an exceptional rail journey through some of Northern Queensland's iconic Gulf Savannah landscapes. The train only carries a small number of passengers, so you will experience a friendly atmosphere which adds to the pleasure of the train. Morning tea is served during the tour and the guide keeps you entertained with species identification, amusing stories and colourful characters.

The Westlander

The Westlander train is a must for train trekkers and future train trekkers alike. Once you begin your journey, you leave the hustle and bustle of everyday life behind as you travel on. A comfortable journey with appetising meals offered in the Club Car is a chance to meet fellow travellers. You have a choice of first class economy seating and sleepers. Depending on the travel sector, a complimentary in-seat snack pack will be delivered to each seat at meal times. Light refreshments can be purchased from the Economy lounge. It's an unforgettable journey which takes you into Queensland's western frontier as you follow in the footsteps of the early pioneers while watching the striking scenery pass you by.

This scenic journey from Brisbane travels across the Great Dividing Range and through the rich farmlands of the Darling Downs before arriving in Charleville, the largest town in the south-west.

Charleville, population 3335 as of the 2016 census, is situated about 750 kilometres drive west of Brisbane, and has a lot to offer. The heritage trail leads visitors to the town's many historically important buildings, while the Bilby Centre provides rare encounters with the endangered marsupial. Charleville, with its wide pretty streets has a number of attractions. There's plenty to do that appealed to me as well. Life carries on at a docile pace and I was soon embracing the everyday culture. The locals meet at one of the outback's best pubs, the Ellangowan Hotel, to catch up and chat to visitors who come across it. It is the kind of place where you learn more about the way of life in the bush than you would in any galleries. One of my fellow travellers told me that Charleville is often overlooked by travellers who make straight for the more popular places like Winton and Longreach. I sat around a fire pit to hear how Indigenous Australians read the stars without any of the hyperbole. Charleville was surveyed as a township in 1868; it has been part of Gowrie Station. Charleville is best known for its bilbies, its clear starry skies and a World War 11 history that's as strange as it is vague.

It is also home to a large Royal Flying Doctor Service Base and a major distance education centre, the heritage-listed Hotel Corones – built in the 1920s by Harry "Poppa" Corones, a Greek immigrant who had arrived in the country moneyless - as well as a fascinating failed experiment in the form of the Steiger Vortex Rainmaking Guns. The Steiger Vortex gun is a cone-shaped barrel, fabricated from sheet steel, designed as a rainmaking device. It was originally designed by Albert Steiger with the aim of preventing destructive hailstorms in a wine growing region of Austria. The firing of the cannon-like device caused a discharge of gas which set up vibrations in the clouds, causing rain. It was failed attempt at producing drought-breaking rain. Drought was and is a constant problem in Australia and in the 1880s a number of rain-making tests had been attempted at Brisbane's Eagle Vale Racecourse. These included, firing high-powered rockets into clouds, balloons conducting electricity to and from clouds and salvos of artillery fired from 10 cannons into clouds. All were spectacular failures.

In 1943, 3500 US Air Force personnel descended on the town to work on classified missions at one of the most secret military bases in Australia. They travelled to Australia on the Queen Mary and eventually to Charleville where they were housed in tents. In addition to the Airforce units, many United States Army forces embarked in Australia, using it as a base of operations prior to their deployment to New Guinea in 1942 and other islands in the Southwest Pacific, driving the Japanese forces north towards their home islands. Throughout the Pacific War, Australia remained an important base of operations, but with the advance of the Allied Armies, the air-bases were returned to the Royal Australian Air Force once the Allied Forces deployed north during 1942 and 1943.

I eagerly followed a tour of the base to learn more about the assignments here in the outback. I was completely surprised to find the size of the former top-secret American Air base on the fringe of Charleville, and is now the heart of a new interactive hands-on exhibition which reveals the region's covert role during World War 11. Charleville was the mustering point for the B17 bombers for the Battle of the Coral Sea. 250 Flying fortresses arrived in Charleville for pre battle maintenance and flew to Charters Towers for refuelling and loading the bombs. In 1942 the Charleville Airport Compound was handed over to the USA Army Aircorp Division to establish the secret base.

Respected woman in the town, Mrs. Adrian, whose parents were certainly to be considered pioneers, and whose mother made some remarkable journeys on horseback, with pack-horses as baggage transport, always took a keen interest in the welfare of the town, and was a foremost organiser of social functions in aid of charitable and religious institutions. The first hotel was owned by a Mr Cooper, who, later sold out to Mr. Louis Gantzke, Mrs. Adrian's father; this was opposite where the Commercial Bank now stands; Mrs. Adrian lived there until quite recently, and is the owner of the property. Her burial place was on the sand-hill where the Catholic Church was later built.

The survey was made by Surveyor Tully, and was named Charleville after his native town in Ireland; Alfred Street he named after the Duke of Edinburgh, who was then visiting Australia; Galatea Street he named after the ship in which he came to Australia, and Edward Street after the then Prince of Wales, later King Edward. The names of explorers, Bourke, Wills, Eyre and Sturt, were given to cross streets. What a history! The first teacher was Mr. Bunce who taught in a hut where the School of Arts now stands. John Armstrong was one of the first to be president. Gowrie was a sheep and cattle station, and the Hon. Walter Flood was the owner; he built what was then a fine house and made his residence there; this house is now the Boy's Hostel. The cattle slump in 1920 was not greatly felt by the district as the price of wool was very high. In the drought of 1900, the value of mulga had been well demonstrated, and those in the wool and stock business looked upon the Warrego (the Warrego River is part of the Darling catchment within the Murray-Darling basin which is located in the Orana region of New South Wales) as the safest pastoral country in Queensland.

The stars belong to all mankind, and we all relate to them in different ways, whether as beacons of light for navigation, as basic calendars, remembered loved ones, or to share stories of heroes and villains. When the opportunity came up for me to be able to view the night sky up close and personal, I just couldn't refuse. The Charleville Cosmos Centre, dedicated to ensuring visitors enjoy the wonder of the outback night sky, offers a focused look at our night sky, and with the outback's low luminance, there's no better place to do so. You wonder at the breathtaking spectacle of the Milky Way, binary stars, planets and the Moon or you can savour seeing solar flares with their special solar scope during the day. My goodness, heavens to Murgatroyd, ahh and brilliant are the words you hear as visitors view the incredible Milky Way Galaxy through powerful telescopes. I left with an appreciation of the beauty and magnitude of our amazing galaxy.

Australia is a huge country and the best way to appreciate its vastness is to cross it at ground level, in comfort, by train. Now a rest from train trekking? Well, planning for the next rail escape at least, won't go amiss will it.

Adriana Carboni
Sydney 2024

REFERENCES

Eyre, Edward, 1865, viewed 19th July, 2021. https://www.museumoflost.com/aliens-on-the nullarbor.

Aussie Towns, ND, Burra SA, viewed 10th October, 2021, https://www.aussietowns.com.au/town/burra-sa/burra/05aa

Tandanya National Aboriginal Cultural Institute, 2020, naming, viewed 18th August, 2021, https://ampww.en.freejournal, info/14777878/1/Tandanya-National-Aboriginal-Culture.

Adelaidia, ND. Viewed 4th August, 2021, https://adelaidia. history.sa.gov.a/places/tandanya.

Ausemade, 2017, Port Augusta SA, viewed 8th October, 2021, https://ausemade.com.au/destinations/south-australia/port augusta/.

Rowe, Peter, 2017, ABC Rural, https://www.abc.netau/ news/rural/2017-03-22/peter-rowe-outback-mail-carrier.

Flinders, Matthew, 1802, Aussie Towns, viewed 28th September, 2021, https://www.aussietowns.com.au/town/kangaroo-island-sa.

Wanderlust, 2018, Urban to Outback: Crossisng Australia on the Indian Pacific, viewed 30th July 2021, https://www.wanderlust.co.uk/content/australia-outback-train-indian-pacific

Wikipedia, 2021, Nullarbor Plain, viewed 5th October, 2021, https://en.wikipedia.org/m21/nullarbor/_plain

Royal Flying Doctor Service, ND. John Flynn Biography, viewed 15th September, 2021, https://www.flyingdoctor.org.au

Tench, Watkins, 1788, Aboriginal Life Through European Eyes, viewed 10th September, 2021, https://www.aboriginal-heritage.org/history/history/

NSW Government 2016, State Archives & Records, NSW Anzac Centenary.

Oakes, John, Sydney's Central, 2012. The History of Sydney's Central Railway Station.

Hyatt, Rob, ND. Koorie Heritage Trust, viewed 14th September, 2021, https://www.visitmelbourne.com/regions/melbourne/meet-the-makers/rob-hyatt

Carboni, Raffaello, 1854, Things That Made An Impression, viewed 20th August, 2021, https://thingsthat made an impression.wordpress.com/2017/03/04/exerp-from-the-eureka stockade

Coober Pedy History, ND. Viewed 14th July, 2021, https://www.cooberpedy.com.au/coober-pedy-history/

Aboriginal Heritage Office, 2008, A Brief Aboriginal History, viewed 1st October, 2021, 2nd paragraph, https://www.aboriginalheritage.org/history/history.

Munro, Jenny, ND. A Brief Aboriginal History, viewed 12th August, 2021, https://www.aboriginalheritage.ore/history/history/

NSW Government, State Archives & Records, NSW Anzac Centenary, 2016.

Wikipedia, 2020, Yarra River, viewed 29th September 2021, https://en.wikipedia.org/wiki/yarra_river

Oakes, John, 2012, Sydney's Central, Australian Railway Historical Society, New South Wales Division.

Lynnie, Trevellian, 2015, A Bit of History, viewed 7th September, 2021, https://www.pinkroadhouse.com.au/travellers/

Noske, 1930, Growing Up Next to the Todd, viewed 3rd August, 2021, https://www.abc,net.au/local/stories/2007/12/02/2114817.htm

Waters, Neil, 2017, Meet the Cameleers Behind the 'Melbourne Cup' jof Camel Racing, viewed 21st September, 2021, https://www.abc.net.au/news/2017-02-07-15/alice-springs-camel-cup/8697596

McPhee, 2017, Australian Rangers warn tourists of significant crocodile threat, viewed 30th September, 2021, www.xinhuanet.com//english/2017-02/18/c_136065829.htm

Burke, 2019, Zero Deaths, but 'deadly' salties exist unde-tected in the river, viewed 2nd October, 2021, https://www.katherinetimes.com.au/story/6463306/

Uluru-Kata Tjuta National Park, The Olgas or Kata Tjuta? Viewed 29th September, 2021, https://parksaustralia.gov.au/uluru/about/the-olgas-or-kata-tjuta/

Wikipedia, 2021, Arafura Sea, 22nd September, 2021, https://en.wikipedia.org/wiki/arafura_sea.

Aussie Towns, ND. Rockhampton, Qld, viewed 15th September, 2021, https://ausietowns.com.au/town/rockhampton-qld

Place Names, 2021, Rockhampton, viewed 14th September, 2021, https://placeandsee.com/wiki/rockhampton

SUMMARY

I wrote this book to share the excitement, spirit and adventure of long-distance train travel in Australia. I hope that train trekkers and future trekkers alike will enjoy reading this book as much as I enjoyed writing it.

Adriana
Sydney 2024

BIOGRAPHY

Adriana was born, and grew up in Sydney (in the year that won't be revealed). She joined Westpac bank and spent a good part of her career in the banking industry. She holds a Diploma in Modern Languages (Japanese), a Bachelor of Arts majoring in Italian and Japanese and a Diploma in Library Studies and Information. She wrote this book to share her experiences gained during these travels, and did her writing during these journeys and at her home in Sydney, transporting readers to lush and untamed lands of this ancient continent, and bringing the lifestyle of warm and fascinating people to these stories. She continues to travel by long-distance trains whenever time permits – and it usually does.